DANNA'S DUST

A Cancer Warrior's Journey
First Edition

Danna Wessels

10-10-10
Publishing

Publisher
10-10-10 Publishing
Markham, ON
Canada

Printed in The United States of America

Table of Contents

This book is dedicated to all of the members of the Cutaneous T-cell Lymphoma (CTCL) listserv. I reached out to them shortly after my diagnosis of CTCL stage 1A. From the very first response I received, to the friendships built over years, these people were a constant lifeline to me in times of both despair and celebration.

Foreword

When I met Danna Wessels in 2014, we were both invited speakers at a conference sponsored by the Cutaneous Lymphoma Foundation. We had an immediate connection. Not only did we share the experience of being CTCL and stem cell transplant survivors, I loved her energy. That energy—her openness and positive spirit—definitely come through in the book you now hold in your hands.

Danna describes with such honesty and humor some of the biggest obvious trials of a CTCL diagnosis. Her fellow patients and their loved ones can testify to the challenges of accessing treatment from a physician who knows the disease. My first oncologist actually pulled a volume down from the shelf and said, "Let's read and learn about this together." You can find a breast cancer specialist in almost any city, but it can take some time to find physicians who really understand the various presentations of CTCL. I also saw myself in her descriptions of how cancer can steal your precious resources of time, money, and purpose. Like her, I had to travel long distances—sometimes to another state—to receive treatment, and felt the worry of expensive medications and the loss of work that comes from symptoms like skin redness, peeling, itching, and skin tumors.

Perhaps the most important aspect of this memoir is her open, encouraging account of the less obvious challenges. Cancer does not just take a toll on the body. It wears on the mind and on the soul, too. Danna's poems express that struggle beautifully, and her suggestions for keeping an affirmative, confident attitude are simple yet meaningful. Having lost my own husband to cancer, I also have a loved one's perspective and was very familiar with her descriptions of Nancy's struggles. Clearly, Danna and her partner Nancy have been there.

What cancer patients need most, no matter what their specific condition, is hope. For almost all of us, the first thought after hearing the diagnosis is, "Oh god, it's cancer. I'm going to die." We need to hear it over and over: There is hope. We need hope to accept treatment, and hope to invest in our own health and well being, and hope to fight when things get hard.

As a registered nurse, when I talk to people about CTCL, I tell them, "Cancer is Cancer." But this disease is rare, and many people haven't heard about it. They hear the word "cutaneous" and say "Oh, skin cancer. That's not so bad." Those of us who have had CTCL touch our lives know it isn't skin cancer and it can cause great suffering. We also know how frustrating it is to see all those pink ribbons and yellow wristbands, and feel lost in that crowd. There is still so little research and funding dedicated to CTCL. Books like this are necessary if we're going to convince the medical community and the public that cancer is indeed cancer, and that all patients deserve help fighting for their lives.

Like Danna, my memoir was my first ever attempt to write a book; I too felt a strong need to share my story. I can tell you...it seems to take forever! It's not that easy to get all of your thoughts together, reaching into memory to get the sequence of events right, and make everything work for the reader. I stuck with it because I felt I had to. I wanted to give people like me hope when they felt alone and lost in the crowd. So I can tell you that *Danna's Dust* is not just a noteworthy accomplishment, it was written out of a desire to uplift others. If you or someone you love is suffering from CTCL, and you're wondering if you can get over the hurdles in your path, there is inspiration in these pages for you.

Foreword

Danna's cancer journey and her truth are, of course, not exactly the same as my cancer journey and my truth. Your journey and your truth will be as unique as you are, too. But there is hope, wisdom, and encouragement here for everyone. I hope you find it.

His Mercy Endureth,

Donna Hussey, R.N.
Author of *His Mercy Endureth*, nurse, and CTCL survivor

Solitary
Danna Wessels

It's dark. Very quiet for those in attendance.
The stage lights, low and subtle under the curtain.
All spectators have placed the programs under their seats.

Little light bulbs above the music sheets catch my eye.
Ruggedly handsome bearded man in tux signals the orchestra.
Deep, heavy, intense, painful first notes are played.

See the sweet light in the crease as the left curtain recedes left.
The right curtain recedes right.

Male dancer center stage lying flat on unseen gorgeous abdomen.
His tights are nude, and chest, too.
His arms rigidly straight, outstretched above his head with thick coal black hair.

A rush of passionate notes hits our ears
While seven large wood whirligigs descend upon the stage.
They twirl and whirl while the beautiful male lies beneath them.

Now. Seven dancers—no—eight, moving fluidly, arms flapping up and down.
Whirligigs are whirling, beautiful male is lying lifeless.

Dancers, one behind each other, enter the whirligigs
Moving swiftly, weaving in between the seven, the child's toy, the whirligig.

One by one. Dancer becomes whirligig. Whirligig becomes Dancer.
They merge. Peace fills the performance center.

The beautiful male lies lifeless all the while.
Beautiful, beautiful Boy.
No whirligigs.
No merry-go-rounds.

Introduction

In August, 2007, my partner, Nancy, and I were busy running through the woods, climbing a high ropes course, giving our best primal screams, and walking over hot coals. We were mid-way through a 5-day Enlightened Warrior personal development camp, in the beautiful Catskill Mountains.

We woke early to have coffee and a little time together before another busy, physically and mentally challenging day. We were preparing to meet the rest of the group for yoga, and I had just stepped out of the shower. As I stood in the middle of our hotel room toweling off, Nancy gave me a long, strange look. "Danna," she said, pointing to my abdomen, "What is that? It looks like a rash."

I looked down. She was right; there were a couple of dry red spots. "I have no idea," I replied. "I haven't noticed them before." I had plenty of other things to think about. My fingers felt like pincushions from the blood sugar tests I had to do before any new activity. With all of the physical challenges, we were both exhausted every night. And neither of us was certain what would happen next. I just wanted to finish my coffee in peace before another crazy day. "Maybe they came up overnight. Anyway, I'm not feeling any discomfort," I said. "Let's get on with today and worry about this later."

"Ok," she said doubtfully. "But when we get back to Austin, we're making you a dermatologist appointment."

Years later, after all I've been through, I can recall a particular moment on the first day of that camp, well before Nancy noticed anything odd.

It happened during the first 15-minute introductory talk. One of the guides said, "Be prepared! This course can change you at the cellular level." In the moment, I thought, "Great. There are certainly some cellular issues in my body that could use rearrangement." Little did I know that the instructor's words would soon turn out to be more accurate than any of us could have guessed...just not in the way I had in mind.

When we got back to town, I made that doctor's appointment. The dermatologist took a look, and said, "Hmm...could be eczema. I'm not sure, but let's start there." She gave me a prescription, told us to change our laundry detergent, and said to check in again if things didn't get better soon. But the red patches went nowhere. Two weeks later, back I went.

"Any improvement?" she asked.

"Nope."

"You used the steroid cream every day?"

"I did."

"Switched to a laundry detergent for sensitive skin?"

"Yes."

"Ok, I think it's time for a biopsy." She took a little sample of tissue from each patch and promised to phone with the results in about five days. When that call finally came, the dermatologist's voice said, "Danna...I regret to inform you of this, but the biopsy results are in. It's Cutaneous T Cell Lymphoma, Mycosis Fungoides." The diagnosis was cancer. Changes at a cellular level, indeed.

Introduction

My name is Danna Wessels. At the time I was diagnosed with CTCL, I had been living with chronic health conditions for years. First, I was diagnosed with Juvenile Diabetes in 1998; then with Addison's Disease, in 2004. I was no stranger to living with a compromised immune system. For most, CTCL is a very slow-growing cancer, so it looked like this was going to be one more thing I had to learn to manage while I got on with living my life. During that call, my doctor had said, "It's far more likely that you will die *with* this than *from* it. That's how it is for most people with CTCL. You will just have to do ongoing maintenance treatments to keep it from moving into your blood."

Nancy and I thought, "Well, this is another thing we'll have to learn to deal with. We're used to it." We had adjusted to life with six to eight daily blood sugar tests, an insulin pump, adrenal insufficiency meds, and anxiety avoidance strategies (Addison's makes it hard for my body to respond to stress.). This was one more long-term health concern, and we would find a way to juggle it with the others.

Except the cancer had other plans. If, like me, you or someone you love has received a cancer diagnosis, I'll bet you have discovered the same thing we did about this disease: it *always* has other plans, so you'd better be prepared for anything. In my case, it was a far cry from the occasional *maintenance treatments* that Nancy and I were told to expect. My journey led through four stages of increasingly aggressive treatment to a life-saving stem cell transplant that completely replaced my immune system.

Like me, every cancer patient—and every supporter, like my amazing Nancy—is on a unique, individual journey. Nobody else's symptoms and treatments will be exactly like yours. There are things that bond us together, however. For me, connecting with a network of other CTCL patients was almost as big a lifesaver as the transplant. Sharing stories, treatment pros and cons, and encouragement kept me going through some very dark times.

I did get through it. Sometimes, thinking back, I still get emotional remembering the challenges I faced. But at the end of that long, difficult path, when I was cancer free, planning my wedding to Nancy, and on the cusp of a beautiful new beginning, I saw again how much that patient community had meant to me. I could also see it was my turn to give back. It started with a few speaking opportunities through the Cutaneous Lymphoma Foundation, and slowly grew into the book you now hold in your hands.

This is my story, and I'm sharing it for the sake of anyone dealing with a cancer diagnosis, particularly those dealing with CTCL. All forms of Cutaneous T Cell Lymphoma are rare, and they get a lot less attention and funding than more common diseases like Hodgkin's Lymphoma or Leukemia. Sometimes it's easy to feel like you're alone in a sea of pink ribbons. I'm here to say that I understand, and this book is most especially for you.

Chapter 1

Whose Body is This Anyway?
– Taking Control of My Cancer Journey

"All the adversity I've had in my life, all my troubles and obstacles have strengthened me...you may not realize it when it happens, but a kick in the teeth may be the best thing in the world for you."
– Walt Disney

Stage 1A

"Danna," said my doctor, over the phone, "I regret that I have to inform you that the biopsy shows you have Cutaneous T Cell Lymphoma. Mycosis Fungoides."

I froze. The only word of that sentence I had recognized was "Lymphoma." *I have cancer?* I could feel myself starting to panic.

Her voice was soothing, "It's Stage 1A. That's the first stage, which means we caught it early. It's rare, but it is also very slow moving. In fact, I'd say you're much more likely to die *with* this disease than you are likely to die *of* it."

"What does that mean?" I asked, breathless.

"It means it is very treatable. I'll refer you to a specialist. They will get you on a schedule of treatment and hopefully get things stabilized quickly. We need to focus on keeping the cancer cells from invading your blood stream. After that, you should be able to manage with regular maintenance treatments and live a normal life."

By the time the call was over, I had mastered that initial fear. The prognosis my dermatologist had described was not an immediate death sentence, and I was already living with two, long-term health conditions. I have lived with Type-1 (Juvenile) Diabetes since 1998. A few years after I got that diagnosis, I developed Addison's disease, a hormone insufficiency that occurs when the adrenal glands fail and the body can't make enough of certain hormones, like cortisol. When that illness set in, I spent more than a year dealing with exhaustion, depression, and weight loss. I never felt like I could get enough sleep. I was foggy and sluggish. I had almost no appetite, though I would get weird salt cravings and devour handfuls of dill pickles or olives. I would even drink the juice from the jars. My insulin levels sometimes seemed impossible to control. It was 14 hellish months before we finally got the correct diagnosis and a successful treatment routine.

After surviving those two crises, the doctor made CTCL sound like a walk in the park, so Nancy and I felt we had reason to be cautiously optimistic. It was just one more thing we'd have to add to the mix in my healthcare routine.

That didn't mean we weren't going to take things seriously. Even at Stage 1A, cancer is something you have to tackle head on. A cancer diagnosis can feel like a total loss of control. Your own body has turned against you—it's the most powerless feeling in the world. So I made a choice: I may not have had control over developing the cancer, but I was certainly going to control my response to it. In many ways, that's the key during the first stage of a cancer journey, whether the illness is a slow mover, like CTCL, or a more aggressive, fast-moving type. It's about deciding what you can control, and then seizing control of those things. In my experience, this boiled down to three basic *control steps* that Nancy and I took during those early days, which set the tone for our whole journey.

We knew the first thing that had to happen right away. It was a lesson we had definitely learned from my past experiences of illness: **The first step is to find a great doctor.**

Control Lesson 1: Find a Great Doctor

First, let me say that I'm not suggesting general practitioners can't be top-notch physicians. Many people get their initial diagnosis from the GP who has taken care of them for years. I mean developing a relationship with someone who has extensive experience with your particular disease. To win a cancer battle, you need someone who knows everything there is to know about your illness, and who has helped others to beat it.

What makes a great doctor? It isn't just about expertise, though obviously you want someone who has in-depth knowledge about the disease, how it progresses, and current treatments. No matter what life-threatening condition you might be facing, you absolutely want to make sure that the physicians on your treatment team are highly skilled, well informed, and reputable. You can and should ask other doctors about a provider's reputation, research their professional history, and interview them about their knowledge and their philosophy of care. They should also have a network of affiliated care providers, such as hematologists, oncologists, and dermatologists, who also specialize in treating your specific disease. Expertise is the first criteria, however, not the only one.

Bedside manner is important, too, of course. Nancy and I already knew how frustrating it is to deal with someone who is cold, or unfriendly, or impatient. (In the later stages of my treatment, we would experience at least one example of an alarming communication failure. I'll share that in a later chapter.) When you are sick, and your loved ones are worried and stressed, you feel incredibly vulnerable. The last thing you want is someone who seems completely detached or uninterested in your situation. If a doctor gives you a bad vibe, or the personality fit is just wrong, it's okay to ask for a referral to someone new.

In addition to expertise and personality, it's absolutely vital to find a doctor who will listen to you. I can't stress this enough. Your physician may be the world's smartest guy, and totally charming too, but if he doesn't have time for your questions, beware. Your questions, your concerns, and your opinions matter. Remember, in the end, you are the person who has to endure all of the treatments that others prescribe.

I was incredibly fortunate in my lead physician, Dr. D. The dermatologist we chose is the guru of gurus for T-cell mediated skin diseases. She has a 30+ year track record, and people come to her from all over the world. She has cared for more than 2,000 individuals with cutaneous T cell lymphoma. She set up my treatment plan, helped me find the dermatologists who had the right equipment, and explained how she would manage my case. She was incredibly thorough. Dr. D. even had me visit a medical photography lab at the hospital to have head-to-toe pictures taken. It was no Glamour Shots session, believe me. The whole thing was pretty weird and awkward. But it gave her a photographic map of my skin so she could track any changes that might occur.

Dr. D. sent us back to Austin with a game plan in hand, so my regular dermatologist knew exactly which steps to take. With those recommendations, my local doctor was able to immediately reach out to the medical community and find a colleague who had the specialized equipment that my treatment required. I was scheduled to start almost immediately.

With a strong, supportive team of doctors in place, it's time for the next step: **find a network of people who know what you're going through.**

Control Lesson 2: Find a Great Network

Another thing I did right away was find the Cutaneous Lymphoma Foundation (CLF). I also found the CTCL listserv, a peer-to-peer network for Cutaneous Lymphoma. We signed up immediately. It turned out to be the best move I could have made.

The thing about CTCL is that it is a tough cancer to explain to people. Everybody knows what liver cancer, breast cancer, or lung cancer is. But tell them, "I've got Mycosis Fungoides," or, "I've got Cutaneous T Cell Lymphoma," and they say, "Huh?" Of course you don't want to show them, because your skin looks like you've got a terrible case of eczema...or mange...or leprosy. No one wants to see or hear about a serious rash. They mostly just edge away from you and wonder if you're contagious.

And, honestly, even for those who do have a better-known, less visually off-putting form of illness, it is still hard to talk about it with people who haven't been there. It isn't that you try to keep your diagnosis a secret from family or friends, but most of them can't do more than offer sympathy. They don't understand the disease; they haven't experienced your symptoms, and they don't know what goes through your mind. Other patients do.

With a rare cancer like CTCL, there often isn't a good local option for a support group. But modern technology made it possible for me to meet others all over the world. If I hadn't been connected to such a great, generous community through the CTCL listserv, I don't know how I would have made it through the standard first stage treatments, let alone everything that followed.

The standard initial treatment for CTCL is a prescription steroid cream. Almost every CTCL patient starts there, and sometimes that's enough to alleviate the problem. If the prescription cream doesn't do the trick by itself, they progress to UV-B light exposure, which involves an initial series of multiple treatments a week, over the course of several months, and, then, ongoing intermittent visits throughout the year. For many, that is enough to keep the cancer in check for life.

Here's how it works. At the dermatologist's office, they usher you into a changing room, and you strip right down to your birthday suit. You put on a terrycloth robe, then scuttle down the hallway, hoping there are no other patients in your path.

At last, you arrive at the light booth. Off comes the robe. You're now totally naked. Woman or man, the technician gives you foam pads to cover your nipples, to protect them from the UV rays. (Guys, you also get a thick sock to put over your dangling buddy.) Everyone also gets a pillowcase to pull over their heads—they say it's for the UV, too, though it feels more like something to cover your embarrassment. You stand in the booth and flip a switch to let the technician know you're ready to go. The technician turns on the juice, and your body is bombarded with UV-B rays for 15–60 seconds. When that's done, the technician releases you from the booth, and you scurry back to the changing room to get dressed.

Once it's over, you hustle back home as quick as you can, to put on pure aloe gel or a paraben-free moisturizer, just like you would if you'd forgotten the sunscreen during a day at the beach.

Fellow patients on the listserv helped me keep my sense of humor about those treatments, and to endure the symptoms that followed. The UV rays cause a reaction—sort of like a nasty sunburn. The skin tightens (I could feel it starting on the car ride home after each one), flushes red, and then the itching begins. And, oh, the itching. I had never experienced anything like it. It was constant. It was severe. It got worse after every treatment. I think I would have gone nuts if it hadn't been for the understanding and tips from my patient network. They were the ones who told me to expect more angry red patches to pop up after treatment began, so I didn't panic when things seemed to get worse instead of better. They told me to expect up to eight months of symptoms before life got back to normal, which sounded unbearable at the time but helped me keep realistic expectations. When I or another CTCL newbie would post, I would read their responses:

"Just keep slathering on the steroid cream."

"Get a paraben-free moisturizing lotion."

"Try having someone coat your whole body with aloe vera gel."

"Eventually, you'll only have to do this a dozen times a year, just like us."

And, most important:

"We've all been there. Don't give up."

Finally, after months of being nuked like a frozen burrito, the red patches went away. My skin cleared up and started to look normal again. The itching stopped. My network was there to celebrate with me...and they would be there later, when the cancer made its next attack.

Control Lesson 3: Create the Right Attitude

This should probably come first, but if you've been diagnosed with a serious illness, you know that things can start happening so quickly. Between the shock and the constant stream of doctor's appointments and tests, the early days pass in a blur. It can be hard to get your thinking right, because you likely haven't had much chance to think at all. So, the first chance you get, stop and take a breath. I was fortunate in this respect: Nancy and I have enjoyed attending personal growth seminars for years, so I had a lot of opportunity to practice positivity and right thinking, before my diagnosis. Believe me, it made a big difference throughout my journey.

Cancer, even in a manageable form like CTCL 1A, tries its best to take things from you. It seems to target the things you enjoy most, the ones that give you joy and keep you in a positive framework. For example, I love swimming laps. On days when I was sad or scared, the ones when I cried over the frustration and unfairness of having cancer on top of everything else, I would swim. It really helped. Then, shortly after I started the UV booth treatments, I had to stop. The chlorine was too hard on the many patches that had come up on my legs, back, and abdomen. It would have been easy to give in to anger and bitterness. Instead, Nancy and I started taking neighborhood walks together. We focused on mindfulness—enjoying each other, the beauty of our neighbors' flowers, the weather, the physical movement—anything to stay in a place of gratitude and light.

Next, it starts to pick away at your privacy. Here's a basic cancer fact for you. Prepare yourself. You will soon be spending a lot of time naked in front of strangers. This will probably be true, no matter what type of cancer you're fighting. I was mortified enough having to wander around a doctor's office in just a robe; I had no idea that was just the beginning.

Our social life was cancer's next victim. As the treatments went on and the rash intensified, my skin began to flake in clouds of dust. Most CTCL patients experience this, and they can tell you it's almost as awful as the constant itch. My skin fragmented into my clothing, coated the surfaces of our home, and powdered the interior of our car. We did our best to laugh, making jokes about *Danna Dust,* but it tried even Nancy's incredible patience. Some days we'd be driving, and she'd look at the dashboard in disgust, and sigh, "I just wish you'd quit getting your dust all over my car." Eventually, we had to stop going to concerts, or movies, or just out to dinner. The dust followed me everywhere, and the itching was relentless.

Even showers, one of life's simplest pleasures, became a chore. The routine depressed me: wash with the special gel soap; put on one special lotion before turning off the water; hop out; apply more moisturizer. And the doctors even wanted me to change how I put that on. I had to rub in a little, wait, pat it dry with a towel, and repeat. If I wasn't careful, my body would be totally gooey with those creams and unguents, and my clothes would stick to me, and it just felt awful.

Even in the early stages, cancer can change your life in ways that are very hard to accept. That's why attitude matters. Let me break it down for you:

First, it's how you discipline yourself not to focus on all of the inconvenience and discomfort you're experiencing.

Second, it helps you find and appreciate any blessing you still have, which is a talent you can keep and use for the rest of your life.

Third, it opens you to the gifts that humility has to offer. Dignity and pride don't hang around when you spend half your time naked in front of strangers, scratching obsessively, and trailing clouds of your own genetic material. When I became humble, I started to see the places where I needed to grow as a person. And there's no reason cancer should stop anyone from doing that.

Fourth, it allowed me to ask for the kind of help I needed, and see clearly where I needed to go to get it. It's funny; most people sincerely want to help when they find out you have a serious medical condition. The problem is, most of the things they do aren't really much help at all (A chemo patient, with no appetite, doesn't want another casserole, thank you very much.). And they never know what to say, so they constantly say the wrong things. By keeping my attitude right, I was able to find the people who were in the best position to offer encouragement and guidance: my fellow patients on the CTCL listserv. I was also able to ask my friends and family—the *outsiders* who didn't have the experience to relate but wanted to be there for me—for the things that actually made a difference. During the years of my journey, I ended up asking for many things. I requested rides to and from treatment when driving would have been impossible for me. I called them for assistance when I was in terrible physical pain while Nancy was at work. I accepted family offers to come over and slather me in aloe vera or wrap me in hot towels.

Finally, the right attitude enabled me to fight. Every cancer diagnosis is the start of a war, and every patient must be a warrior if they want to survive. There will be times when the inconveniences crush your spirits, the physical pain makes you scream, or the fear drives you out of your mind. I have experienced all of those things. Some days were incredibly hard because so much seemed to be going wrong, and it was all out of my control. I could control my will to live, however. I could choose where I focused my energies. I could decide whether I embraced the hate I felt for the situation, or the love I received every day. It was up to me to decide which voice in my head to listen to— the voice of fear or the voice of hope. I chose hope.

When Cancer Comes Calling

Life after diagnosis, when the tests and treatments start, can be overwhelming for everyone involved. Patients struggle to come to terms with the idea of fighting an invisible enemy that has invaded their bodies. Loved ones strive to be strong while trying to master their own fear and uncertainty about the future. Friends and colleagues want to help but have no clue what to do. Everyone feels lost and out of control.

Let me remind you of the first and most important discovery I made on the path to beating CTCL: **None of us had control over how we ended up on this path, but each one of us can control how we respond.** Embrace that, and let it guide you through the journey.

My hope is to help you restore your freedom of choice when cancer tries to take it away from you. For that to happen, it's critical to act quickly and decisively in the three control steps; so, be bold in:

- Choosing great doctors.
- Choosing a great network.
- Creating the right attitude.

If you're reading this, as a patient or a caregiver, there are many things you can do to make the journey easier. You just have to choose confidently to do them:

Embrace your right to make decisions about care. Medical professionals are necessary allies, but the needs/desires of the patient and caregiver matter too.

Find people who get what you're going through. There are disease-specific support networks—local and online—for both patients and caregivers. Take advantage of those. If face-to-face meetings feel uncomfortable, join a listserv.

Ask for help when you need it, and tell people the kind of help you need. You don't have to force a smile and take yet another frozen lasagna if you don't want it. Let people know if you need a ride to treatment, or a break from being the patient's driver; or a trip to the nail salon, or a box of popsicles.

If you're reading this as a friend or supporter to patients or caregivers you know, you can make good choices too. Here's how:

Listen and sympathize if they need to vent, without trying to solve the problem. Believe me, they don't want to hear someone else say, "Everything happens for a reason," or, "I'm sure you'll be back on your feet soon." Stick to, "That sounds really tough."

When you offer to help, ask what is needed. Don't assume they want flowers, or food...or anything! Unless you're a survivor yourself, don't send unsolicited gifts, which may end up being a burden rather than a joy. Let them off the hook when it comes to thank you cards. They have enough to worry about without feeling like they owe you.

If they ask for space or privacy, honor that wish. Even if they don't say it, if you get that vibe, listen to your instincts and back off. You can send a card or e-mail to let them know you're thinking of them and you are there if they need help.

As someone who's survived the difficult ordeal, I can tell you there's no one right way to *do cancer*. However, I can also tell you that a mindful beginning can reap benefits later on. I certainly saw the results of my early choices when my disease progressed to the next level.

"The Law of Attraction and its magnetic power reaches out into the universe and attracts other thoughts that are vibrationally like it... and brings that to you. And so, you are getting the essence of what you are thinking about, whether it is something you want or something you do not want."
– T. Harv Eker

Notes

Notes

Chapter 2

A New Normal...or Not
—Navigating the Obstacles in My Path

"Storms make trees take deeper roots."
– Dolly Parton

"We're Not Getting a Sustained Remission"

About a year into my CTCL treatment, Nancy got an exciting job offer in Colorado. It was a great promotion opportunity and a chance to live in the foothills of the Rocky Mountains. I was doing well with regular UV-B treatments, so we decided to grab the chance. We moved to Boulder, in July of 2008.

At first, everything seemed to fall right into place for this new chapter in our lives. Nancy liked her job. We loved the city. The weather was great, and we enjoyed walking the dogs in the cool new neighborhood. My Austin dermatologist helped me find a local office with the right equipment. I got a part-time job at the Barbara Davis Juvenile Diabetes Center. I found a yoga class. The patches cleared up, and my skin started looking and feeling better. Nancy and I thought we'd settled into the new normal.

 And then the patches came back. Both doctors and listserv friends had said this could happen. They said the condition could wax and wane, and that it might take up to eighteen months before achieving *sustained remission,* the point where the cancer was really kept in check. So, I didn't worry; I just kept showing up for my dates with the booth technician and his pillowcase. We tried for another nine months. At last, my new hematologist, Dr. M., looked at me and said, "Danna, I'm afraid this isn't working. We're not getting a sustained remission."

Of course, I was frustrated. I'd been on the CTCL listserv for over a year, reading about the people who got through the initial phase and then plodded along for decades, getting into the UV-B booth twice a month and getting on with their lives. I wanted that to be me. So, I had to look myself in the eye and say, "Ok, Danna, you're not going to be in that percentage. It's a setback, and it's disappointing. But how you respond is up to you."

I could already see that my attitude was going to be a key factor in the next step. I have to thank Nancy and my Granny for helping me put it into words: **Focus on what's happening for you, not to you.**

Attitude Lesson 1: Focus on What's Happening for You

When I was a child, my grandparents owned a barbecue restaurant in Northwest Houston. My granny's pies were a customer favorite. They were so popular that some regulars would eat dessert before ordering their lunch so they wouldn't be too full of chopped beef sandwiches to enjoy a slice of pecan or pumpkin.

One Christmas, when I was about 10 or 11 years old, Granny and my mom decided they could use that talent to make a little extra cash. They put an ad in the *Houston Chronicle,* offering holiday dessert catering. Anyone who wanted scratch-made pies for Christmas parties, holiday dinners, or to give as gifts, could call up and place an order. Any number, any flavor—Granny would deliver. Granny and Mom imagined some dedicated customers would tell a friend or two, the phone would ring a few times, and they'd make a couple dozen pies and a little money for presents. Instead, the phone rang off the hook for 3 weeks solid.

It was like an episode of *I Love Lucy*. Hundreds and hundreds of orders came in. Granny, Mom, and Mom's sister, Carolyn, had to set up an assembly line in both the restaurant kitchen and Granny's personal kitchen. They baked night and day. They scrambled around, chopping, mixing, and rolling out dough; moving pies in and out of the oven; packing them up in cardboard boxes and hand writing the customers' names on each one.

When it was over, they were all exhausted! The last thing they probably wanted was to make Christmas dinner or more pies for their own family. But here's what else I remember: in the middle of all that chaos, they still had a lot of fun. They could have gotten angry at themselves for biting off more than they could chew, or mad at each other when things felt beyond their control. They could have complained about what was happening to them. Instead, they focused on the opportunity, and on enjoying each other's company. Sure, it was stressful, but their attitude allowed Granny, Mom, and my aunt to work together in an efficient, organized, and upbeat way.

Years later, when we confronted the fact that the UV-B wasn't working for me, Nancy said, "Danna, try not to focus on what's happening to you. Think about what's happening for you. We don't know why this is happening, but this experience will serve you in some way."

I think back on that Christmas, and I see that's probably what got my family through the crazy pie ordeal. They didn't see it as bad luck happening to them. It was an opportunity to be together, have some fun, and raise a heck of a lot more money than they had imagined!

So I kept doing my yoga, listened to positive intention CDs in my car, and meditated constantly on that thought: How are these obstacles and challenges going to serve me? What will I learn that make me a better, happier, and more thankful individual?

I was going to need that affirmation during the next round of treatments, which brought their own lesson: **Some things are: Just. Plain. Hard.**

Attitude Lesson 2: Know That Some Things Stay Hard

Steroid cream and UVB treatments are first level responses to CTCL. If they don't control the cancer, you have to move to more aggressive methods. My doctor's next choice for me was nitrogen mustard cream, aka "chemo in a tube," as my listserv friends liked to call it. It is crazy expensive, and is derived from mustard gas, the chemical weapon developed for WWI. Believe me, it felt like chemical warfare on my skin. They say to start by applying a very thin, light layer on the patches, then slowly work up to a heavier dose. I have no idea what a thick layer might have been like, because on the third or fourth day of putting it on, I thought someone had lit my legs on fire. Nancy was at work, and the pain was so bad I had to call a friend. He picked me up, took me to his home, and wrapped my legs in ice packs. That was my last date with Nitrogen mustard cream. I am just glad I didn't end up in the emergency room on a morphine drip.

If the chemo in a tube isn't viable, the next step is often photopheresis. It's a little like a tanning booth for your white blood cells. A machine pulls a small quantity of blood out of your body and separates it into the different components. Then it treats the white blood cells and platelets with a photoactive drug and zaps them directly with UV light. The machine pumps the treated fluid back in, then starts over with a fresh batch of blood.

The upside of photopheresis is that it doesn't drain your energy during the procedure, like a lot of cancer treatments. In fact, you just lie still and nap, listen to music, or watch movies. But, honestly, that's about the only pleasant part of the procedure. To start, it takes 2.5–3 hours once they get the blood draw started. Add to that the time it takes to get to and from the hospital, the check in process, and the post-procedure wait time, and that's pretty much your whole day. Then there are the headaches. When they take that much blood out of your body, the blood pressure often drops, causing painful headaches and dizziness. I was fortunate that I didn't experience that too often, but many people in my network did. And then there's the needle.

Lord, those needles! I'm an insulin-dependent diabetic; I deal with pricks and sticks and injections on a daily basis. But I'm not talking about those tiny, skinny things you see when you get inoculations. Photopheresis requires a 16-gauge monster. I thought it looked like a soda straw. It makes such a big punch hole in the skin that it can leave scars. It goes into the main vein in the crook of the arm. For me, it hurt like the dickens, *every single time*. And I had to endure it twice a week for nine months. They had to switch back and forth between my right and left arm to give the puncture marks and veins time to heal. And if they didn't get it right the first time, it would continue to sting for over half an hour, which meant they had to pull it out and try again on the other side!

I have to be honest: Photopheresis never, never got any easier. It was just as hard the last time as it was the first. My nurse, Michell, tried on every occasion to make it more bearable. She was funny, and she had a cow squeaky toy she called *Miss Moo*. She'd crack jokes and squish Miss Moo to make her go *squeak-a-squeak-a-squeak*. She'd talk to me like I was a fussy baby in a photography studio: "Look at Miss Moo! Look over here, Danna!" Michell tried her best...but that needle still sucked every single time.

And it sucked when they pulled it out and mashed on my arm for what felt like forever, to stop up the puncture wound. And it sucked to wait for the blood, seeping out of the giant hole in the vein, to clot so I could go home. It sucked when I had to be helped to the bathroom afterward because I was too weak to walk that day. It sucked when the treatment itself was finally all over, but the itching started up.

It sucked having to wear cotton gloves at night so I wouldn't scratch myself raw in my sleep. It sucked when cancer took away a position I loved and that allowed me to help others. My part-time job involved helping the parents of newborns get their babies' umbilicord blood tested for the Type 1 diabetes genetic marker. I treasured working with the families, and it felt good to know I might be helping these children avoid the suffering I had experienced through being misdiagnosed. Then, as my skin reacted to the photopheresis, my lab coat became a torture device. My body felt like it had fire ants crawling everywhere while I was at work. Plus, if I got a fungal infection on my skin, I could be a health risk to these fragile babies. So I had to quit. If you've ever lost or had to leave a job that gave you real satisfaction, you know how desolated you feel sitting at home in the aftermath.

It was all just really hard.

That's a difficult truth about dealing with CTCL, or any cancer, or any life-threatening illness. Some things are just hard. They don't get easier, no matter what you or anyone else may do. So you have to be careful. Attitude actually matters more in the face of the unavoidably hard things, not less. If you don't control your mindset, the trials—things like a 16-gauge needle or a long night of feeling like you've got fire ants on every inch of skin—start to take over your whole brain. The obstacles become so large and intimidating that you can't see or think about anything else, and your days fill with fear and dread. That's when you must remind yourself to look for what's happening *for* you. You can't avoid the suffering, but you can choose to focus your eyes on the light at the end of the tunnel. It's there, always. Concentrate on that, rather than pain, frustration, or the disappointment of failed treatment routines. I made myself focus on the things I still had: the beautiful home in Boulder I shared with the woman I love; affection and devotion from our sweet corgis, Gracie and George; the amazing people on the listserv who knew exactly how I was feeling and were always ready to offer words of wisdom and support. I chose to put my energies where they could still have an impact: journaling; taking care of my body; using those hours hooked up to the machine to write, answer e-mails, and work on my computer.

That positive, assertive outlook not only helped me stand up during tough times, it was essential to **standing up for myself with my healthcare providers.**

Attitude Lesson 3: Tell Your Providers What You Need

We all hoped that 9 months of photopheresis would get my body back on track, but the itching only got worse. It hit me everywhere, from the palms of my hands to the soles of my feet. This happens a lot with CTCL patients; I even heard about a couple of the people who were driven to suicide by the unrelenting discomfort.

The symptoms became so severe that only one thing gave me any relief: heated wet wraps. Like so many of the things that helped me most, this suggestion came from the listserv, from several of Dr. D.'s patients who had tried it at her recommendation. We would put a plastic sheet down on the family room couch, run super-hot water into the kitchen sink, and put towels in the water. While they soaked, we would rub my entire body with prescription steroid cream. Then, when the towels were ready, we would put a layer of them on top of the plastic, and I would ease my body onto the scalding towels, face up. Then, someone would hurry over with more towels to cover me from head to toe. I would lie still for about 20 minutes, wrapped in a tight, damp, warm cocoon. That would soothe the itch for about 24 hours, then we'd have to start again. Our household water bill went sky high. The photopheresis obviously wasn't working, and I asked Dr. M. for a break in the treatment so we could contemplate what to do next. For the next couple of months, we would check in with visits and routine tests.

At last, Dr. M. scheduled an appointment with us. "I'm sorry, Danna. The disease has progressed from Mycosis Fungoides to Sézary syndrome. That means it has moved into your blood. We can try a couple of other things first, but I think we should get you on the list for a stem cell transplant."

We agreed, but thought it would be a good idea to check in with Dr. D. Nancy and I flew out to meet with her, and we were shocked to hear her say, "Your Diabetes and Addison's are hard enough to manage when you're otherwise healthy. I'm not saying not to do it, but you need to know you could die. I think you should try Interferon before you go down that road."

I still remember the walk out to the car after that appointment. We were disappointed, distraught, and confused. We were in the parking lot before Nancy and I realized we hadn't pushed back at all. We hadn't asked her any questions. It was clearly a busy day in her office. We decided that when we got back home, we'd go straight to Dr. M. and see what he said.

We did follow up with her suggestion, doing research on the treatment and asking for advice on the CTCL listserv. The information was not encouraging in my specific case. Many of my patient friends responded, "Ugh, interferon is awful. It's like having a really bad flu for weeks." And the results could vary widely. Some saw improvement, while others thought it was no help at all.

Medical providers, even the ones on the same team, can have disagreements about prognosis and treatment options. That's not necessarily a big deal. What counts is making sure that, as patient and caregiver, your voices are heard too.

So, back in Dr. M.'s office, I said, "I've checked out the interferon that Dr. D. recommended, and it does not sound like a good fit for my situation. We feel very strongly about giving it a pass. I really want to get on the transplant list."

He agreed, "It's the right choice. Even with your compromised immune system, you've got a good chance of surviving and thriving."

We asked him to be the one to share our decision with her. "How do we get Dr. D. on board?" Nancy asked.

"I'll schedule a conference call. There will be a lot of doctor talk, so I don't think you need to join in. I'll let you know how it goes." He called and kept it simple, just as we requested. "Danna doesn't want to do the interferon shots. Nancy doesn't want her to do them, either. Because it has such a small percentage of success, my office doesn't think they should do it. They prefer to move straight to the transplant, which I agree is the right choice." In the end, Drs. D. and M. agreed that a transplant, following a rigorous plan of TSEB therapy, was the best path.

I was fortunate in that I already had some practice pushing back when a doctor's recommendations didn't feel right. My local dermatologist, who had overseen the UVB light treatments, had recommended PUVA light treatments when the photopheresis didn't do the trick. Nancy and I looked at the option. But the pills involved in PUVA are famous for causing nausea, and the statistics didn't show that it helped in a majority of cases. I am incredibly prone to nausea; if it's a listed side effect for a medication, I'm sure to get it, and I don't tolerate it well. So, I told this doctor I was going to take a pass on the PUVA. She was not happy about it, not one little bit. But, as the patient, the decision was mine to make, and I said no. I didn't like what I read about interferon, and I knew it wasn't a good choice for me, either.

Perhaps I would have ended up on the transplant list even if Nancy and I hadn't stood our ground. But God knows what I might have had to go through if I hadn't stood up and spoken out. That's the third lesson about attitude, and it's not just about being positive and hopeful (though those things give you strength); it's about knowing you have the right to tell your healthcare providers what you need.

It's your life. You get to choose whether an option is right for you, and how far a treatment goes. If you want a change, ask for it. If something doesn't feel like a good fit, say "No." Nobody's going to live forever, and you have a say in the quality of whatever time remains to you.

When It Don't Come Easy

Life can get frustrating and scary if you have to step up treatment. It's easy to feel bitter that first level treatments didn't work for you, and to resent other patients who *got off easy* by comparison. I admit that sometimes I envied the people who just had to go stand in a light booth a few times a month. It is also tempting to give in to dark thoughts, to worry that it might get worse, or despair that the pain and discomfort may never go away. I encourage you to master those negative impulses quickly, by practicing these three attitude checks:

- Focus on what's happening *for* you.
- Know that some things stay hard.
- Tell your providers what you need.

Just like when you took the first steps of your cancer journey, a patient or a caregiver has a number of opportunities to be proactive:

Take every opportunity to enjoy small pleasures. Count your blessings. Find things you can work on. Maybe you can't change the fact that you itch, or are in pain, or feel tired all the time. Find a personal change you've wanted to make—one that is in reach—and make it. Maybe that's writing regularly, or letting go of an old grudge, or learning French. Prove to yourself that you can still do *something*.

Keep sharing your thoughts. Advocate for your needs and desires with anyone who threatens to steam roll you, whether it's a doctor, nurse, social worker, friend, or partner.

If you're reading this as a friend or supporter to patients or caregivers you know, here's how you can help at this stage:

Respect their suffering. Don't say or do things that minimize pain or discomfort. This doesn't mean you have to indulge self-pity, or listen to constant whining, but let them express how they feel.

Back them up in the choices they make about their healthcare. This can be tough, especially if they refuse or discontinue a treatment that you think might save their life. Remember that they have to endure it, not you.

Feed them encouragement. Remind them that they are still funny, smart, insightful, or anything else you have always admired. If they show growth or personal development, find a simple, non-patronizing way of complementing them.

While Nancy and I were walking the difficult path of my CTCL treatment, I can tell you there was never any substitute for mindfulness. The slow, complicated process of diagnosis for both Type1 Diabetes and Addison's disease had given me plenty of practice in making my voice heard with medical professionals. Looking back, I could finally see how those situations had happened for me, just like Nancy said.

At this point, we couldn't deny that things sometimes got dark, and that there would probably be moments that would be darker still. But thanks to our years of personal development, right thinking, and meditation, we were also experienced at looking for the light. That's exactly how we got through what came next.

"When you face difficult times, know that challenges are not sent to destroy you, they're sent to promote, increase, and strengthen you."
– Joel Osteen

Notes

Notes

Notes

Chapter 3

Burn, Baby, Burn
—Killing My Immune System to Save My Life

"Strength does not come from winning. Your struggles develop your strengths. When you go through hardships and decide not to surrender, that is strength."
– Arnold Schwarzenegger

Hold the Sugar

No type of transplant is simple. Whether it's bone marrow, a heart, or any other body part, the process involves taking material from Person A's body and putting it inside Person B, where it will be treated as a foreign object. There's a lot that can go wrong. The immune system doesn't like foreign objects; its whole job is to keep them out. That gets even more complicated when the illness lies in the immune system itself, as it does with all types of lymphoma.

One of the things I most respected about my doctors was their refusal to sugarcoat the facts. Before transplant, Dr. M. was considerate, but he made things clear. In my case, he laid out the seriousness of the situation: if I didn't get the stem cell transplant, I probably had 2–3 years left to live—and I'd spend them red, irritated, and itching. He said, "I'm not God, and I don't know everything, but I've treated other patients who have gotten to this stage. The disease is in your blood now; and with that full body rash, you're highly susceptible to infection. If you don't have this procedure—even if you do keep up

29

with your current treatment regimen—you've probably got 24 to 30 months." It was shocking to hear him say it. After all the talk about CTCL being something people died *with*, it was the first time I really feared it was something I might die *of*. Out of over 500 people in the listserv network, only 3–4 had passed away in the time I had been a member. They had the rarest type of CTCL, which presented with painful, oozing tumors. Mentally, I had always put them in a different category. Now, holding Nancy's hand and listening to Dr. M., it hit me: *I might not survive.*

There was still significant hope, he said. If I did get the transplant, I had a strong chance of a full recovery, even with my complicated health history. But to get those new cells, first I would have to endure a miserable ordeal. He explained in detail, drawing pictures as he went. To save my life, I was actually going to have to have a whole new immune system, grown from someone else's stem cells. To keep my white blood cells from shouting, "Look out, guys, foreign object!" then stomping those cells like a cockroach in the kitchen, the doctors were going to have to *boot down* my existing, diseased immune system. In other words, they were going to have to burn it to the ground. This would involve a lengthy treatment period to pave the way, and would include both radiation and chemotherapy.

At the end of the meeting, Dr. M. handed us some pamphlets and a list of resources where more information could be found. He asked us to consider the facts for a few days and then come back to him with a decision. Then he told me something I didn't expect: **The whole truth may not be good for you.**

Survival Lesson #1: Decide How Much Truth You Can Handle

"Danna," he said, "The process of doing the research and analysis for aggressive treatment can be scary. Given your body's inability to handle stress, I don't think you should be the one to do that. Nancy is better equipped." He suggested that she dive into the research and get the full picture. After that, as a couple, we could decide how much she should share with me. It may seem counterproductive, maybe even ethically questionable, to keep a patient in the dark. But for me, it took a terrible burden from my shoulders. Dr. M.'s advice taught us something valuable: **As the patient, you have to decide how much truth you can handle.**

It was hard for Nancy to confront the full picture, to learn all the risks and the struggle involved, and to decide what to keep to herself. I'm eternally grateful that she carried that burden for both of us. It ended up being the right choice. The next steps were hard enough on my body and my mind. It would have been even worse if I had known exactly what was coming and had to face it filled with dread.

If you are preparing for an aggressive procedure, you may feel differently, of course. It could be that you need a lot of information to feel empowered and prepared. That's fine. My point is that you have to decide how much truth is good for you. If you want all the facts, demand them. If you need a little distance from the hard parts, take it. If your closest loved one or caregiver can't deal with the responsibility, find someone who can.

Knowing your truth level also makes it easier to cope with the pauses and delays that can happen at this stage. The odds are good, **you're going to be doing some waiting, and you need to find ways to make it bearable**.

Survival Lesson #2: Whistle While You Wait

My medical team got me in touch with Chris, the registered nurse who coordinated the transplant process. She explained that the first step was to run the tests that give them the necessary information about blood antigens. Any stem cells put into my body would have to closely match mine, or my body would simply reject them. They could then test close family members to see if any of them were viable donors.

Unfortunately, in my case, my sister Terri was the only possible choice. We soon found that she was not a match, and none of my other relatives were good candidates.

When the family option didn't work out, the next step was registering my profile with Be the Match, a large non-profit that helps thousands of people find bone marrow donors each year. They keep databases—one for the U.S., and another international. After that, Nancy and I could only wait. The system would let Chris know when a donor's profile seemed like a good match for mine.

Waiting is never easy. Whether you're anticipating something good, or worried about something bad, sometimes it feels like the waiting alone will kill you. And when you need a life-saving procedure, like a transplant, it actually might. There were days when it was hard for us both not to obsess about when a match might be found, and whether it would happen soon enough. That kind of waiting can lead a person to flip out, believe me. When you obsess over something—when it takes over your thoughts, and your mind is spiraling out of control—that's called mind friction. It was at this point that Nancy and I could see there were going to be plenty of occasions for mind friction on the road ahead. Focusing on the positive, and living in the moment, were going to be more important than ever. Basically, **it's about learning to whistle while you wait**.

One perk of waiting for major cancer treatment is that the doctors generally want you to gain some weight. Aggressive treatments hit the body hard, and most people lose 20 lbs. or more in the first hundred days after a stem cell transplant. For me, this meant I got the chance to live a little. Between the Diabetes and the Addison's, I typically have a very strict eating regimen. And, like many others, I'd been told "cancer loves sugar," and had to make further adjustments to my diet when I began CTCL treatment. While waiting for the transplant, however, the doctors told me to live it up...well, comparatively speaking, anyway. We were urged to go out to eat as often as we liked.

I was supposed to enjoy rich foods to help with my weight gain. Dr. M. even said, "If you want a margarita, have a margarita. If you want a glass of wine, drink it." For someone who is insulin dependent, that sounds downright hedonistic!

So, Nancy and I concentrated on living a little. I ate things I enjoyed. She changed up her exercise and diet routine so she could increase her energy. We played with our dogs. We made the most of evenings and weekends when she was free from work. Even though I was itchy, I took pleasure in having a break from uncomfortable treatments. Those things definitely kept my spirits up during the hard days of waiting. It helped me keep my equilibrium when Chris called to tell me that my first donor match had backed out of donating when she learned about the 16-gauge needle they would use to draw her blood. Nancy reassured me, "That woman just wasn't intended for you. Your perfect match is out there." We whistled while we waited.

Then, at last, Chris called and said, "We've got a donor. She's from the Netherlands, and she matches on all 10 antigens." It was time to move to the next step. Now would begin the fight that truly tested my mettle, and demanded that I **call on the warrior within.**

Survival Lesson #3: Find Your Inner Warrior

While we were pausing treatment and waiting for a donor match to come through, Dr. D. grew concerned that my fragile skin would become vulnerable to infection. That could have been disastrous. She accepted the need to discontinue UV-B light therapies, but insisted I make a daily habit of vinegar washes as part of my shower routine. This was both simple and awful. I kept a gallon jug of plain white vinegar in the bathroom. Every day, after I finished washing and turned off the water, I had to pour a mixture of vinegar and H_2O over my whole body. Smelling like a pickle would have been unpleasant enough, but the excruciating sting was worse. Imagine falling asleep at the beach and getting the worst, most blistery sunburn you've ever had in your whole life. Now imagine getting up the next morning with lobster-red, swollen skin, and pouring something acidic over your naked body. Imagine doing it every single day. I would stand in the shower, dousing myself with vinegar, screaming as I poured.

I was certainly glad that I got to discontinue those vinegar washes when it came time to begin Total Skin Electron Beam therapy. Of course, if I'd known everything about that process, I might have said, "I'll take the pickling instead, please."

Total Skin Electron Beam (TSEB) is like something out of a sci-fi movie. It starts in a hospital changing room, where you put on your gown. This is not the typical, butt-baring, cotton hospital gown, though. It's synthetic, construction worker yellow, and see-through. You look like something out of an '80s music video. Next comes the long, long walk from the changing room, through hospital corridors, to the radiation auditorium. If you're lucky, they give you something to drape over the plastic gown. Next, you meet up with a medical technician who puts anesthetic drops in your eyes. After fifteen minutes, to make sure your peepers are totally numb, they carefully and slowly insert a set of lead contacts into your eyes—lead, as in the heavy metal. These are to keep your eyeballs from being fried during treatment. After the contacts are in place, the technician uses medical tape to seal your eyelids closed, to keep your eyes from twitching and being scratched by the contacts. While they work, you're vaguely aware that more people are entering the room.

Then they take your robe, leaving you in just the see-through gown, and there's the 15-foot march to the actual platform, which stands about 4 feet high. You can't see anyone on the way, of course, but you're very aware that they can see you. The technicians guide you, help you find your way up the stairs, and carefully place your hands and feet into a specific, fixed position. They then remind you, "Now don't move!"

Now you can hear voices and the tapping of feet. That's the staff running for the control booth. I used to play a game with myself. If the shoes went *click-click-click,* I knew a female doctor was moving. If I heard *clomp-clomp-clomp,* it was a man in motion. I would try to guess how many men and women interns were present.

Though you can't see a thing, you know you're at the end of a very long room. In the middle of the room, on the right-hand side, doctors and technicians observe from a control booth. In that booth with the doctors, two professional physicists calculate and supervise the settings for the beam; the machine has been set for the exact joules required. The technicians move a large, see-through plexiglass tower into place; it protects you from overexposure. Once this screen is in place, they scramble for the booth. A voice comes over the loudspeaker, "Are you ready?" Remembering you aren't supposed to move, you try to stay stiff and still as you call, "Yes." They turn on your soundtrack, whatever music you've chosen to accompany your TSEB experience, and then they hit you with the radiation. It lasts about 50 seconds, which doesn't seem like a long time until those waves of energy roll over you. Then it feels like forever.

Once that's done, the clicking and clomping starts again as everyone pours out of the control booth. The technicians scramble over and put you in a new position. And they do it all again. You're up on the platform, blinded, posing like a pole dancer to your personal soundtrack, with all your girly (or boy-ly) bits on view for everyone to see. After 3 rounds of zapping, the technicians help you down from the platform, assist you across the room, and liberate your eyes. You get your robe back, and you make the thousand-block walk back through the corridors to the changing room.

You go through this four times a week for 10 weeks. It's such a grueling process that some people actually drop out of treatment. They can't tolerate being handled by so many people, or they get claustrophobic, or the beams are more than they can bear. It takes mental and emotional resources that not everyone has.

Then comes a brief break. In my case, for two weeks, I rested at home. Right before the transplant, you return to the hospital. A series of tests will determine whether your body can tolerate the final steps. If you pass those, that means you're healthy enough for them to almost kill you. They start off with a little chemo—in my case, 3 bags over a few days—to make sure your immune system has been nearly wiped out. Last, comes one final blast of full body radiation at very close range. For that, you lie on a table, and they hit you with the light. Only then will you be ready for your new stem cells. When they peeled me off the table at the end of that treatment, I was the sickest and most wiped out I have ever felt in my entire life.

This experience made me so glad for all of the enlightened warrior training I had done, because **it was the mental and physical fight of my life, and I had to become a warrior.**

First, the TSEB process was no picnic. The stakes were high, the clothing was minimal, so much could go wrong, and lead contacts just suck—I had to push hard through the mind friction, and find positive thoughts. I found reasons to be grateful. For one thing, all of the red patches went away. Another example: when we were getting the orientation, an intern told us that I would need shots in my eyeballs before each treatment. I looked at Nancy, tears streaming down my face, and said, "I guess I'm going to die, then, because there's no way I can do that 40 times!" Fortunately, the doctor soon came in and corrected the intern's mistake, saying it was only drops, not shots. So, every time they sealed my eyes with tape, I said to myself, "At least there were no needles involved!"

Second, the treatments themselves sapped me of energy and vitality. I would go home after the TSEB, exhausted, with tight, stinging skin. It was all I could do to put on aloe vera gel (with my sister, Terri's help) before I collapsed. I clung to the messages of the musical soundtracks I chose. Whether I was on the platform or lying on the couch, I kept my favorite bands' songs running through my head.

Third, I often looked as rough as I felt. I lost weight. I was pale and pinched. My hair started to fall out. I lost my fingernails, toenails and eyelashes.

After I shaved my hair I embraced the fun of wearing hats. One nice thing my hospital did was provide a collection of hats for patients, many made by volunteers. Every time I went to the hospital, I'd pick something new and cute. Every few visits, we would wash and return the ones I had, and I'd find something different. Cheap entertainment? Maybe. But when you're too nauseated and exhausted to truly give a shit about how you look, embrace whatever small pleasures you find. You'll feel better.

Last, and maybe most challenging, it was hard to be forgiving when the professionals made mistakes. I still remember the day they put my ports in, as one of the worst experiences of the whole journey. It's a small surgery that installs a central line in a chest vein. It makes drawing blood and giving medicines easier because they're not pricking you with new needles all the time. It only takes a few minutes and shouldn't be a big deal. But in my case, scheduling changes moved it a couple of hours after I had a chemo treatment. That meant I had to be lifted up from the table multiple times during the procedure so I could vomit into an emesis bowl. I felt like I might die, and it would have been easy to take it out on them. Instead, I kept myself together. Months later, when I felt better, I was able to write a firm but polite letter to the hospital asking them never to put someone through that again.

Surviving the Kill or Cure Days

When a disease advances to a certain point, sometimes you start to wonder, "Will it take me out, or will the anxiety get me first? Or worse, what if the cure kills me?" It starts to feel like everything is a threat to your survival. Getting through it takes guts. I hope you'll pay close attention to three survival choices, which kept me on the path to beating cancer, and which can help you deal with the inevitable mind friction:

- Decide how much truth you can handle.
- Whistle while you wait.
- Find your inner warrior.

Patients and caregivers can expect to experience heavy stress and adversity when disease progresses this far. I do believe that you can make choices to help you weather the storm:

Decide who should be the *keeper of the information.* Maybe it's the patient him or herself. Maybe it is a spouse or parent, or a good friend, or even a hired professional. Every member of your treatment circle should be honest about how much truth they can handle. Someone needs to know everything there is to know, so figure out who is best suited to the task, and decide in advance how to communicate as treatment progresses.

When you find yourself in a holding pattern, waiting for test results or a donor, do what it takes to find joy and pleasure in the day-to-day. Obsessing and stressing can kill you. Caregivers, this is true for you too; uncertainty can have ill health effects on anyone. Ask doctors what you can safely enjoy. Give yourselves permission to do things you like to do together—things you ordinarily put off with excuses.

Find small blessings to count, even something as simple as, "At least no one stuck a needle in my eye." Cancer will tell you that everything is awful, it can only get worse, and it will never get better. If you stay grateful for small things, you prove every day that cancer lies.

Find your soundtrack. This is another thing that both patients and caregivers should do. Surround yourself with the music that makes you feel good, brings up happy memories, and fills you with fighting spirit. (By the way: this is not the situation for *"my woman left me and my dog died"* type of heartbreak songs. Pick things that make you feel positive and confident.) If movies or TV programs give you those feelings, add those to the mix too. You can also add books. I was often too tired to read, so I went with audiobooks. I couldn't always pay close attention to the story, but it was a good distraction from the pain.

If you're reading this as a friend or supporter to patients or caregivers you know, here's how you can help at this stage:

Keep your questions to a minimum. Patients and caregivers like to know you care, but they get tired of repeating themselves to every new visitor. Also, it makes them feel worse if they don't have answers. Consider setting up a website, newsletter, or social media page on their behalf. That way, you can keep friends and supporters up to date, without the patient or caregiver having to repeat the same news over and over.

If they need to vent, listen. Be ready to say, "That's so tough," or, "I'm sorry you're going through this hard time." No need to say more.

Invite them to ask for the kind of help they need—a ride to the hospital, babysitting the kids or dogs overnight, doing a grocery run, watering the houseplants—there are lots of things that get tough to juggle during aggressive treatments. But let them dictate the kind of help they need.

Respect the need for space. Patients and caregivers may not want the added stress of visitors in their home. If you're running errands or dropping off requested supplies, be ready to leave them by the door. It's nothing personal, I swear.

The kill or cure phase of treatment gets a lot of attention because that's where all the drama is. The stakes are highest, and the medical intervention is at its most extreme, and there's the constant question of whether a life will end. It's no wonder that many people think the journey ends there. They miss an obvious fact: once you've descended and walked through the valley of death, there's still the long climb back out.

"You never know how strong you are until being strong is the only choice you have."
– Bob Marley

Notes

Notes

The Bear Dream
Danna Wessels

The bear was drowning.
No one was willing to help the bear.
The bear had to help himself.
The bear at different times grabbed onto various rocks to try and save himself.
Each of the smaller rocks only momentarily saved him from near death.
Yet they served a purpose so he could catch his breath before the next rapid came.
The bigger island-like rock at the end of the dream offered safer ground once he could get to it.
However, once the bear reached the safer island-like rock, he realized that the water was rushing swiftly past him and he was standing still. He felt left behind.
For a time, the bear was pleased because he escaped death.
Now he wants to go back in the water.
If only the water would calm down.
The bear feels exhausted from his struggle with the rapids.
The bear feels confined by the small space he is given to escape danger.
The bear feels lonely, for no one witnessed his struggle.
No one bothered to help him.

"Don't fight against your struggles. Live with them, and in them, until your body feels the calm after and because of the struggle."
– Danna Wessels

Chapter 4

Sleeping Beauty Wakes Up
—Overcoming the Myth of the Fairy Tale Recovery

*"Make up your mind that no matter what comes your way, no
matter how difficult, no matter how unfair, you will do more than
simply survive. You will thrive in spite of it."*
– Joel Osteen

The Dutch Miracle

After all the drama of my deteriorating condition, and the increasingly
aggressive treatment, you would think the actual transplant would
have been a huge deal, something climactic and slow-motion camera-
worthy. Everything leading up to it—the heart and lung stress tests,
my vigilant endocrinology team monitoring kidney function, the TSEB,
the chemotherapy—was what you might expect to encounter during
the fight for your life. But the actual stem cell replacement? It seemed
a little anticlimactic in comparison.

Many people imagine that a bone marrow transplant involves either
hacking out a slice of someone's bone or scooping out the soft center,
digging a trench in your bone, then cramming a handful of the stuff
into the hole. The reality is something else entirely.

Basically, they prepared a bag of fluid that contained the donor's cells,
processed and shipped from the Netherlands, and hooked me up to
that bag. Nancy and I said a couple of prayers together, put on our

inspirational music, and then they connected the line and started a drip into my port. Over a few hours, the fluid dripped steadily into my bloodstream, introducing those cells into my body. That was it. That was the actual transplant. After that, it would be up to the cells to make their way into my bone marrow, establish themselves, and build a new immune system from the ground up.

That's not to say that the danger was past. A number of things could still go wrong. The donor cells could fail to proliferate. Or any remaining survivors from my old immune system could mount a last-ditch defense, causing my body to reject the cells. Or (and this was the one my doctors truly feared), I could develop an infection that I didn't have the resources to fight off. Any one of those three things could be fatal. Still, after the prehistoric needles, acid baths, total body nuking, and chemical warfare, the transplant was almost...boring.

Truthfully, I wasn't up for much excitement. I was exhausted, nauseated, and emotionally fried. I felt like roadkill. Boring was fine by me. I was happy just to lie in the hospital bed, hold Nancy's hand, listen to my music, and think about how grateful I was to the anonymous Dutch woman whose generosity was going to save my life. I visualized her cells as magic dust or angel dust falling onto my body, replacing the dust of illness that I had been trailing for so many months.

I have had plenty of opportunity to reflect on my donor's gift in the years that have followed. A person who lives halfway around the world, who will never meet me or even know who I am, let somebody stick the equivalent of a sharpened pencil into her arm and sift through her blood for an hour or more, more than once because she wanted to help save a life. That's pretty humbling.

Of course, I don't remember having a lot of deep thoughts then. Meditation and insight typically happen when you have the ability to focus and the energy to think creatively. In the months following my transplant, **I was essentially in hibernation.**

Recovery Lesson #1: Recovery is Hibernation

Anyone who has a truly significant medical procedure can testify: you lose major amounts of time. I don't mean the "oops, I was browsing in my favorite store and an hour flew by" kind of lost time. I mean days, weeks, or months can pass in a total haze. If you have ever come down with a terrible flu on Thursday and have no memories of anything except coughing a lot until the next Wednesday, you've had a taste of what I am talking about. For days on end, there's almost nothing but sleep. When you are awake, you can't really think straight. Between the drugs and the exhaustion, and combination of physical discomforts, you're overwhelmed. Not only does your body demand more rest because it is busy with repairs, your mind says, "Yeah, this is way easier when I'm not conscious." So, like a bear or a frog, you burrow into something soft, and hibernate.

If a procedure requires a long hospital stay, like mine did, it really does start to feel like you're asleep in a cave, shut off from the world. As I explained in an earlier chapter, the success of my transplant depended on knocking out my immune system. That meant that I was going to be totally vulnerable to infections until the new system had time to grow. Even if I had wanted to, I couldn't go strolling around shopping malls or working in our flowerbeds. The world is a big ball of germs, and it would have flattened me in days. For the first month, they kept me in a clean ward on the 11th floor for only stem cell transplant recepients.

It was the kind of place where barriers seal the patients off from the outside world. Hospitals are always big on sterilizing, but this floor took clean to a whole different level. Staff and visitors had to be cleared in advance, and had to go through scrubbing protocols before they walked through the door.

That's where I spent the first month of my recovery. Other than Nancy and the nurses, I saw almost no one. I slept long hours. They woke me periodically to do tests, but when I was awake, I was too weak and nauseated to be interested in much. I just wanted to roll over and go back to sleep.

And that didn't change for the 2–3 months after I got home, either. Occasionally, someone would rouse me to bathe, eat a few bites, or use the bathroom, but that was the limit of my activity. I would request the CDs I wanted playing in the background of my room, but couldn't have followed a TV show if I tried.

By the time I started to emerge from that fog, somewhere in the middle of month 3, I hadn't seen friends in months. I couldn't remember the last time I had watched or read the news. I had no idea what was happening in the world. I thought I knew how Rip van Winkle had felt.

At the time, the physical discomfort I felt while awake occupied most of my thoughts. Later, when my body began to get better, I would start to feel the mental impact of losing so much time—trying to catch up on what had happened in the world and in our social circle, feeling confused and out of the loop.

I'll tell you something, though: **A few hours after they started the stem cell drip, the itch went away. Completely. Permanently. That alone was worth the price of admission.**

Recovery Lesson #2: Recovery is Inconvenient

After almost four years of battling cancer, I knew how it constantly tried to steal your life, piece by piece. Nancy and I had high hopes that the transplant would be our key to taking back everything it had stolen: my health, my physical comfort, our social activities, our peace of mind, and many other blessings we'd taken for granted. After the miraculous day that the itching went away, we had hope that we had defeated the thief at last.

But we didn't expect that the recovery process could take things away too. **It brought its own assortment of inconveniences.** I couldn't get to the bathroom unassisted or bathe myself, so I had to do those things whenever a professional home health assistant or loved one was available to help. There was my independence, gone. Post-procedure symptoms also got in the way of friendships, as I didn't want to see anyone but Nancy during the months I felt sickest. She sometimes felt like my recovery process took me from her, too, because I didn't have the energy for conversation, laughter, or companionship.

After I started to feel more awake and could move around a bit more, a whole new set of inconveniences popped up. I would get really dizzy going up and down stairs. I was often out of breath. My muscles had atrophied from the long period of inactivity, so I was as weak as a baby. My doctors had always joked that I was "the healthiest sick person they knew," because I was able-bodied with a strong heart and lungs. During this phase, I didn't even have much basic mobility. Just lifting my arms to change my shirt could exhaust me more than swimming 2 miles. And it wasn't cancer that had taken that away, but the cure!

For a while, recovery even denied me access to my fur babies, George and Gracie, who had been my single best source of comfort through the whole cancer battle. They couldn't visit me while I was in the clean ward at the hospital, of course. But they couldn't be there when Nancy brought me home, either. You see, the house had to be spotless. Our housekeeper, Delia, had to come clean our home twice a week, and Nancy had to sterilize surfaces multiple times a day, just to keep things safe for my fragile new immune system. So there was no way the dogs could be around during that period. Dogs are wonderful, but they are germy. I wasn't able to see them at all for the first month I was home.

I missed them so much. I understood that I couldn't have done our ordinary activities, anyway; walks would have been impossible, as was getting down on the floor with them to play. But I missed petting their soft fur, seeing their happy faces, and just watching them have fun together.

After 30 days at the pet sitter's house, George and Gracie went to the vet for a pre-homecoming checkup. George was cleared, but Gracie had caught some sort of virus that could endanger me. He got to come home, but she had to wait another two weeks. At last, after two-and-a-half months, we were all reunited. It felt like the family was whole again, and seeing them lifted my spirits out of the depression that had followed me from the hospital. My healing progressed more rapidly from that point on. It made me see that **recovery could be as difficult as disease, and just as taxing to the body and mind**.

Recovery Lesson #3: Recovery is Taxing

Anybody who watches a cancer story on TV or at the movies is probably familiar with the intense points like radiation, chemo, and surgery. As I said in the introduction to this chapter, those are the parts that make for good drama. You know...slow-motion camera shots; sets full of beeping equipment; waiting room scenes full of tense and tearful (but very pretty) people; dialogue full of big, scary-sounding words. That kind of stuff. The problem is, most of those stories either go from the hospital bed to the graveside, or from the bald, sick person on the operating table to the healthy, hairy person running a marathon a year later. They totally skip over the actual recovery because it is boring and tedious for everyone...*especially* the patient. I knew that it would be slow; my doctors told me it would be. They said, "Our goal is to get you safely through the first hundred days." **They didn't tell me how taxing that would be.**

You may wonder, if the worst was over, if the actual diseased cells had been chased out of my body, why did it seem so bad? Because I was sick and tired of being sick and tired. The experience of physical suffering during my recovery was hard, but the mental suffering was worse.

I guess I kind of thought that once the transplant had been done, the really hard stuff would be over. I told myself:

"I'll never have to see those giant needles again."

"No more Danna dust everywhere."

"I won't have to get zapped with UV rays every other week."

And those things were true. I didn't have to do those things anymore. Instead, I threw up so often, I had to keep a pail by my side at all times. I could barely move. I had to swallow 22 pills each day. I suffered frequent, excruciating stomach cramps from the combination of medications. I could barely choke down a few bites of food at a time, because everything tasted sour or metallic, or smelled rotten, or had no flavor at all. The only meal that tasted appetizing was Nancy's homemade potato soup.

Sometimes I would have a couple of good days where I felt stronger and less nauseated, and I would be hopeful that I had turned a corner. Then I would crash and feel terrible again. I can't tell you how many times I thought, "Will this ever truly be over?" When I was awake and alert enough to be aware of exactly how shitty I felt, I wondered how much more I could take.

Nancy sometimes felt at the end of her rope too. In some ways, this period was harder on her than the time before the transplant, because I was so completely helpless. I couldn't be left alone, but she often couldn't be there to supervise my care. She still had to bring her A-game at work; now would definitely not be the time to get laid off. So, in addition to managing projects and staff at her demanding job, she had to take on the coordination of care shifts, which were split between home health professionals and volunteers. When she was home, she was either cleaning or helping me. Every Sunday night, she had to make a giant pot of potato soup, just to make sure I wouldn't starve the next week.

With a major project launch in progress, she had to be in Boston at least twice during my first hundred days. At first, my sister, Terri, was around to help out, but the idea of flushing my ports every day was more than she could handle. She was terrified she'd get it wrong, and the sight of blood in the tube freaked her out. They ended up having a terrible fight about it, and Terri was on a plane home the next day.

Shortly after that, during one of the Boston trips, I got a serious infection and ended up in the emergency room. My friend, Theresa, who was looking after me in Nancy's absence, was the one to sit at my bedside and make the phone calls with status reports. It stressed Nancy out that she was so far away and couldn't help, but we were both so grateful to Theresa and her husband, Vic.

Theresa, who had been through CTCL and a stem cell transplant as well, would sometimes reassure us that things would get better a little at a time. She was right. Some things I could appreciate in the moment, and others I noticed in retrospect:

During the first two months, I had to see the doctor twice a week. That meant being dragged out of bed, driven to the hospital, then dragged back home. In month three, we cut back to once a week. In month four, it was every other week. At six months, we shifted to monthly visits. And each time, the visits were a little less draining.

My hair began to grow back.

After the second month, the dogs got to come home, which improved my mood a lot.

As the weeks passed, I grew more alert and could watch movies and listen to audio books instead of sleeping constantly.

In month three, I started being able to get to the bathroom and shower on my own.

By the fourth month, my taste buds began to recover and my appetite improved.

I got to the 100-day mark, and my doctors were very pleased with my progress.

When I developed a second infection, it wasn't nearly as severe as the first, and I recovered much more quickly.

At around 6 months, I could take short walks with Nancy in our neighborhood.

I was able to drive by myself again in the seventh month.

In month eight, my ports came out for good, thankfully!!

There were still some extremely uncomfortable, difficult situations. I was susceptible to stomach cramps for as long as I had to take so many pills. The bouts of pain didn't stop until my doctors cut back on my meds. I also hated bone marrow extractions, which involved drilling a hole into a pelvic bone and using a needle to suck out some liquid, to see how well the new stem cells were grafting. Those felt horrible.

Through those long months, I just tried to direct my brain toward positive, hopeful thoughts, and to keep the mind friction at bay. I may not have had much strength or energy, but what I had I poured into that. Every night, we would listen to Carlos Nakai's flute playing, which lifted my spirits and gave me a feeling of peace. When I was awake, I meditated, prayed, and set positive intentions. I constantly thought about the new stem cells—the magic dust floating in my veins. I directed encouragement and healing vibrations at those Dutch stem cells. I silently thanked the woman who gave them to me, and the medical staff who were working together to save my life; I wished blessings and positive outcomes for all of their lives. I was grateful that Colorado had legalized cannabis, because medical marijuana gummies and beverages gave me the most relief from pain and cramping. When I saw how many blood draws they did every week, I was even grateful for the darned ports, because I was sick to death of needles.

I believe my positive thinking and gratitude paid off, and in some unexpected ways. It's our philosophy that if something really lousy happens, you just wait and watch. It may be today, or next week, or a year later, but something good will come out of it. About 9 months after my transplant, Nancy was scheduled to attend a conference in Puerto Rico. "Let's see if the doctor will approve you to travel with me," she suggested. That sounded like the most wonderful idea in the world, so we asked. After they conferred for a few days, then checked and double-checked me out on everything, they gave their approval. The only limitation was that I couldn't swim in the ocean. A chlorinated hotel pool would be ok, though, which was enough for me.

I got to take my first post-transplant flight, with my partner next to me, feeling like a captive who'd just been set free. When we got to the hotel, they made a mistake with our reservation, and Nancy was ready to give somebody a piece of her mind. But I was still high on my newfound sense of freedom, and I was happy to chat with the hotel desk clerk. She noticed I was a type 1 diabetic and told me her mother and aunt were too. I told her about my cancer battle, and we bonded over long-term illnesses. In the end, she upgraded us to a bigger suite, right by the pool. I had wondered so many times in the last two years if life would ever be good again. At that moment, it was very good indeed.

100 Days and Beyond

If you or someone you care about has to go through a serious medical intervention like radiation, chemotherapy, or a transplant, you probably want to do everything you can to prepare. Your doctors, other professionals, and your own research will likely give you everything you need to get ready for the big, dramatic events. But they may not be as thorough in discussing the recovery process. It's really not enough to say, "It could take a while." My hope here is that my story can help you set realistic expectations. Keep in mind:

- Recovery is hibernation.
- Recovery is inconvenient.
- Recovery is taxing.

Parts of it are likely to challenge you in ways you never imagined; your patience and your endurance will be tested. If you start building those mental and emotional muscles now, they will be there when you need them.

If medical intervention is successful, then like me, there's a good chance that the patient will soon be on the road to recovery. That road usually has a steep uphill climb, though. Patients and caregivers may find it tries their strength and stamina just as much as the illness did. Here are some of the things that helped me get through the first hundred days and beyond:

Put something positive in the background. For me, that was music by my favorite artists. For a long time, I was too sick to pay close attention to even something as simple and passive as TV, but my subconscious mind still took in the sounds. Yours will too. So, choose something that soothes you, energizes you, or gives you positive vibes. It could be anything from Schubert to birdsong recordings. Invest in a sound machine, or downloads, or an app for your phone/TV.

Ask for the encouragement you need from the people who have been there. For example, I had met other stem cell transplant patients at the hospital and through the CTCL listserv. They were able to sympathize with the pain and remind us that it does get better. If the patient is too sick to call or e-mail themselves, a caregiver can be the one to contact other survivors and request a note or voicemail saying, "I got through this, and you can too."

Find things to be thankful for or happy about every day. This can be a big milestone, like food starting to taste good again, or a tiny thing like a bird singing by your bedroom window.

If you're reading this as a friend or supporter to patients or caregivers you know, here's how you can help at this stage:

Send attractive, handwritten cards with positive thoughts and wishes. If you have kids, you can have them draw pictures. You can make a short voice/video recording of the patient's supporters, and send that. (Note: it might be best to send to a caregiver's phone or e-mail, since the patient may not be up to checking voice or e-mail very often.) Even if a patient or caregiver can't respond, many of us have enjoyed putting up those notes around the recovery room. It really does make us feel surrounded by love and support.

Consider sending a gift card so the patient can buy some new music or an audiobook. When you are alert, but too sick to move around, there's not much to do but stare at the wall. It gets really boring. Some new tunes or stories can be a lifesaver.

Home health care can get very expensive, and many insurance plans don't cover it. If the patient and their loved ones are open to monetary gifts, collect small donations from a group of supporters and put the money toward hiring a home health worker. Even a small break, a couple of hours on one afternoon a week, can be a lifesaver to a primary caregiver.

One Saturday, back in my early 20s, I was out jogging with a boyfriend, Delvin, on a trail in Memorial Park. The wind blew a newspaper page across our path. I could see a big, bold 5x7 classified ad on the rectangle of paper. My curiosity was piqued, so I insisted we stop and pick it up. It was an employment ad from a large company, describing an opening for a personnel recruiter. Lately, I had been feeling restless and ready to move on from my own job. I was bored and wanted to learn something new. As we read the details of what they required, I said to my boyfriend, "Hey, I think I could do this job. I'm already doing some of what it describes, and it pays more than I make right now. I'm going to apply!" I did, and I got the job.

That experience taught me that if you are receptive and willing, life will open doors for you. All you have to do is keep your eyes open and walk through when you see them appear. Even though your path can contain unpleasant surprises (like, oh say, developing cancer), many wonderful things are also waiting for you. Some of my fellow survivors found that a cancer battle, or other kinds of difficult season, made them hesitant to walk through doors of opportunity. Their suffering had made them fearful.

When Nancy offered me the chance to visit Puerto Rico, I knew I hadn't lost my open, willing spirit because I jumped at the chance. I was ready to start living again, and to walk through the beautiful doorways life was about to open for us.

> *"This moment is as it should be."*
> – Deepak Chopra

Notes

Notes

Notes

Chapter 5

Coming Out of the Dark
—Building a New Life After Cancer

*"After your season of suffering, God in all his grace will restore,
confirm, strengthen, and establish you."*
— 1 Peter 5:10

The Past Worst Case

Prior to the long, slow process of growing a new immune system, the onset of Addison's disease was the worst I had ever felt. I still remember the endless, agonizing months of weight loss and exhaustion. I dragged myself through life, lost in a haze of fatigue, memory loss, and depression. My diabetes doctor insisted this wasn't an endocrine problem. It took over a year to get the right diagnosis and treatment routine, and during that time, I sometimes doubted that things would ever get better. What if I felt like this for the rest of my life? What if I couldn't find the energy to be a real partner to Nancy, or take care of our precious dogs? What if I could never swim, or hike, or work in the yard again? What if I faded away before the eyes of our family and friends? Sometimes those thoughts would haunt me and crush my spirit.

Then I got a new, highly skilled endocrinologist who was ready to tackle the case. She solved the mystery, put me on adrenal hormone replacement and tweaked my insulin, and things slowly started to turn around. Without her, I doubt I would still be alive. I still remember the day I realized I was well again. I had stepped into the back yard with the dogs. The sun shone warm, and there was a nice breeze. I was surrounded by green, growing things, and the beautiful flowers in our borders. My body felt light, and my heart filled with this incredible sense of joy. Tears filled my eyes as I threw my arms in the air and shouted to the universe, "I feel better!" What an incredible moment. I had no idea at the time that the discomfort of developing Addison's was just a trial run for the real marathon of misery that CTCL would become. I'm glad I didn't know...but I'm also glad for the lesson that fourteen months taught me: **use it to grow.**

New Life Lesson #1: Use it to Help You Grow

As Nancy reminded me over and over during our cancer journey, "Focus on what's happening *for* you." She still says it when I get stressed out and frustrated. What does it mean? Our brains get focused on the stuff that happens to us—especially when it is bad stuff. When a problem arises or an obstacle comes between you and the things you want in life, it is so easy to chew on those things like a dog chews a bone. If you are reading this, whether you have cancer or you love someone who does, I bet you have said, "Why me? Why us?" more than once. That's natural; it's just what humans do.

But you don't have to live there. You can make a conscious effort to shift your mental focus, and look at the things that are happening *for* you. Consider:

- What lessons can you take away from what you are experiencing? What are you learning now that will help you be a better, more successful person in the future?
- What new, wonderful people are you meeting? Would you have met them if life hadn't put you in this circumstance? What have you learned from them?
- What bad habits, attitudes, or mental patterns has this situation forced you to give up? What positive things would you like to replace them with?

It may be that you're not up to deep thought or meditation on these questions right now. That's okay. I'll tell you what you can do. It's the same thing I did when I was on the uphill climb of recovery, and I talked about it at length in the last chapter. Count your blessings, find small things to be grateful for, and use what energy you have to focus on those positive things.

If you do that, your body and your mind will be ready for those questions when the time is ripe, just like mine were. As my health returned, I felt like a flower opening in the light. I had the energy and mindset to reflect on the things I had experienced in the last few years, and I had so many new insights about myself.

First, I saw how impatient I used to be, and how arrogant I sometimes was in my dealings with other people. Being sick and helpless forced me to wait, to rely on others, and to trust that they were competent to take care of things. I had no choice but to trust! Moving forward, I promised myself that I would take it slow with people and give them the benefit of the doubt.

Second, I realized that, no matter who you are or what your struggle is, there's a community out there waiting to help you. The motto of the Cutaneous Lymphoma Foundation is, "You are not alone." How true that is. Maybe that's one of the miracles of this technological age, or maybe it was always true in different ways. I just know that the CTCL listserv saved my life and my sanity on more than one occasion, and so did local survivors I met and befriended: people such as Theresa Soto. No matter what your problem, ailment, or condition, someone out there has gone through it before you. Thanks to the Internet, you can find them, even if they live halfway around the world. When you are suffering, you are sometimes going to feel lonely. That's true for everyone, and it's not going to change. Again, it's just part of being human. But you are never truly alone. Others have been there, and their basic compassion will make them willing to help you. That's part of being human too. Perhaps, like me, as you emerge from this trial, you will see the universe offers you the great gift of helping those who come after you. I still actively read the CTCL listserv and comment on the threads there. One of my greatest joys is speaking to audiences of CTCL patients, caregivers, and healthcare providers, sharing with them my story and the lessons I've learned.

Third, I had the opportunity to put all of the mental training Nancy and I had undergone to the ultimate test. What's the point of training for a triathlon if you never sign up for a race? You will never see how your hard work pays off unless you find opportunities where it will be needed. On my cancer journey, I had to call on every emotional and spiritual skill I had ever practiced—and some new ones too! Every book I'd ever read, every training or guided meditation recording I'd ever listened to, every seminar and retreat we attended, I used it all to help me get through the fight for my life. And you know what? I made it. That's the best possible proof I could have that those years of commitment and effort had been the right choice. They really did pay off.

So, all of the crappy stuff I experienced during those years? I turned it into fertilizer, and I used it to grow.

New Life Lesson #2: Dream Big and Live Big

Through the whole five year ordeal, Nancy and I actually found **dreaming and goal setting to be one of the most helpful activities we could do together**. We talked about trips we wanted to take. We discussed ways to safeguard and grow our finances (which is pretty gutsy when you think about the cost of medical treatment). We dreamed about crazy big things that we wanted to accomplish, individually and as partners. Some of these were ideas we would have dismissed as too *out there* in our previous ordinary life.

The best example I can give of our big dreams comes from the hardest part of my recovery, when Nancy proposed to me. She said, "Danna, we'll do everything we can to get you well and vibrant again. Then, let's go to New York and get married." Well, who wouldn't want to live for that?

Those dreams kept us going through some really tough times. So Nancy and I felt we owed it to those dreams to make them reality. The months of planning our wedding, in 2012, were some of the happiest and most joyful of my life. My doctors were more than pleased with my progress: I had resumed many of my normal activities, like driving and exercising; and most days, I felt truly well. My body was healthier and more energetic than it had been in years; my spirit felt like it was waking up from a long, nightmare-filled sleep.

Two of our good friends, Carla and her daughter Dori, helped me plan everything. They made me feel like a princess by running the errands and doing most of the grunt work. They arranged things so all I had to do was say, "I want this. I don't like that. Let's go with this one." I had many occasions to be glad that the cancer had taught me to accept help when I needed it. Carla and Dori made the process so easy and so much fun.

And when the moment came, we did it up right. We flew Carla and her husband, David, out with us. We headed for a luxury resort on Long Island in a limosine where we had lovely rooms on the beach. There, on July 31, on a covered deck overlooking the sea, Nancy and I said our vows before a New York judge. We could feel the ocean air on our faces. There were flowers, a violin and piano duo, a cake, strawberries and our favorite champagne, the sound of the waves, and the company of two of our closest friends.

We even had a small, unplanned audience. I've always been friendly, and good at chatting up strangers (remember the hotel clerk in San Juan?). While we were at the resort, I struck up a few conversations: ladies at the hotel salon, people next to us in the lobby, couples walking out on the beach. I told people why we were there. I shared some of the struggles we'd just experienced, and explained how much more meaningful our wedding was to us, after all we'd been through to get here. We were surprised how many of those people responded by saying. "That's amazing! But only two wedding guests? That's not enough! Can I come to the wedding?" Five or six of them actually showed up! Even total strangers felt how miraculous it all was—escaping the jaws of death and walking into the light of a new life—and wanted to be part of it. We were happy for them to be there. It was like the universe had provided us with a little cheering section, free of charge, as we crossed the finish line hand in hand.

After that, we stayed in Manhattan for three nights. We dined out, shopped, and got 4th row tickets for a Broadway show. It was wonderful.

I hope you will give yourself the same gift. Whenever you are struggling, and it feels like cancer (or any other obstacle) will defeat you, find something big, positive, and beautiful to dream. Think of something you've always wanted to do, a challenge you've never dared to take, or an adventure you've always wanted to have. See yourself doing that thing. Imagine it. Picture it in detail. Let that dream fill you with positive energy. Promise that dream: "When I get through this, I'm going to make you a reality."

Then, when you've passed through your ordeal and come out the other side, go for it. Don't talk yourself out of it, or say, "It's not practical," or, "I'll get around to it sometime." Say to yourself, "I've earned this opportunity," and go for it.

It doesn't have to mean spending money you don't have, or throwing good sense out the window, either. Share your dream with others. Go to your network. Ask for advice. Talk to experts. Like those strangers in Long Island, most people are glad to be part of the start of a new life. You can find a way of making a dream come true in the way that makes most sense for you.

New Life Lesson #3: Believe That You are Blessed

Sometimes people come through a trial or tragedy as a shadow of their former selves. It's like the suffering of the past makes them so afraid of future suffering that they become afraid to live. Their bodies may get better, but their souls stay sick and sad. They don't go out. They lose interest in people and things they used to love. It seems like they never smile. Something weighs them down.

With an illness like CTCL, that can be a very real threat. If, like many, the condition is successfully managed at an early stage and kept in check with treatments, a little voice can still pop up in the back of the mind to whisper, "But what if it gets worse some day?" If, like me, a person's long period of pain and misery at last results in a complete remission, that little voice can still creep in to say, "What's going to go wrong next?"

It's strange. That doubt, that fear of experiencing pain again, can make small setbacks and discomforts seem unbearable, even though you know you have already survived so much worse. With my compromised immune system and challenging healthcare routine, you might think that I live in the shadow of such dark thoughts. In fact, the opposite is true. Thanks to the mental training and positive energy work I have done over the years, **I believe that I am blessed, and I live my life from the foundation of that belief.**

When you embrace the idea that you are blessed, and focus on all of the good things life has given you, it becomes much easier to deal with setbacks and disappointments, whether they are large or small. For example, when we held a party in celebration of our marriage, a few key things did not go as planned. Wedding parties are emotional days, and many a bride has felt that her *special day* was ruined by conflict or an unexpected disappointment. Nancy and I never let ourselves be those brides.

Because our actual wedding ceremony took place thousands of miles from our home, and consequently had to be small, we held a grand reception in Estes Park on our return to Colorado a month later. We went all out on the planning (another event in which Carla and Dori were invaluable), booking the Della Terra Mountain Chateau. It was an all-day affair. First, breakfast would be served to a few special friends who would arrive early and help with the setup. An afternoon cocktail hour would welcome the rest of the guests, with appetizers, drinks, and a trio of musicians to keep them entertained, until Nancy and I made our entrance. After some time for mingling, two drummers would enter, playing, and lead everyone down the path to the meadow where an hour-long drum circle would take place. After the drum circle was over, we all would march over the bridge to the Tuscan-style dining hall, impeccably arranged for our event. There would be dinner, a live band named The Fever out of Boulder, champagne and a beautiful cake, and photographers and a cinematographer to capture the whole thing.

All of our friends and relatives were invited: 130 invitations went out, and 102 acceptances came back in. Unfortunately, my mother was not one of them. She went back and forth for weeks about whether she could make it, but then called us to explain that she just didn't feel comfortable with the idea of a same sex wedding. We were terribly disappointed. I'll admit, I cried more than a few tears. But in the days after that phone call, those little RSVP cards kept coming in. It was so exciting to check the mail every day. Instead of dwelling on our disappointment and hurt, we focused on feeling blessed and grateful. We had so many friends who had been there through the cancer battle, and who would be there to support us now. And even if Mom wasn't comfortable with the idea of our marriage, I was (and still am) blessed to know that she genuinely loves me and has had a respectful relationship with my wife. By the time the day arrived, I was so filled with gratitude that I had no room left over to be bitter.

Coming Out of the Dark

In the weeks leading up to the Grand Reception, I also got RSVP cards from some of the nurses who had cared for me during my treatment. I wanted to recognize them in a special way, so I worked and worked on a short speech. I spent a lot of time thinking about it, wanting it to be just right. I considered the length: "I'd better keep it short," I said to myself, "Or I'll get too emotional in front of 90-plus people. I don't want to cry and mess up my fake eyelashes!" I thought about the tone: "Keep it gracious but light. I don't want them to feel put on the spot." I meditated on the words: "I just want them to know how much we appreciate what they did for both of us."

Then, the big day came, and two of the three nurses didn't show. The R.N. who did make it had to leave before the toasts began. In the end, I decided not to make a speech at all. I couldn't promise I wouldn't turn into a big, blubbering ball of tears and snot. So, when Nancy turned to me and whispered, "Do you want to speak?" I just shook my head.

I could have let myself feel hurt or disappointed that I was denied the opportunity to publicly thank my nurses. But it was a great day. Everyone was having a wonderful time. My fake eyelashes were staying right where they were supposed to. When the time came, Nancy and I stepped out on the floor for our first dance, which we had choreographed and rehearsed with an instructor for three months. There was not a dry eye in the house as we moved together to Susan Werner's "I Know What I Want."

At the end of the night, as we slow danced to "The Endless Night," from Disney's *Lion King*, I looked around the room. I listened to the final lines:

I know that the night must end
And that the sun will rise
And that the sun will rise.

No momentary disappointment could overwhelm that feeling of support, love, and joy.

I hope that you will have the opportunity to see all the ways that you, too, are blessed. Live in the light of the good things you have on any given day, and you will arm yourself against any fear or worry over what the future might hold.

Walking into the Light

When you or someone you love emerges from a cancer battle—either through remission or through maintenance—it's easy to heave a sigh and say, "The journey is done." In reality, nothing could be further from the truth. The great journey of your life is still in progress, and surviving the cancer is just part of your story. Post recovery can be a time of great joy; it *should* be a time of great joy. Some are surprised to find that they feel defeated by cancer even though they survived it. If you feel yourself living in fear or anxiety about future suffering, remember these three things:

- Use it to grow.
- Dream big and live big.
- Believe that you are blessed.

It's fine to have down days or periods of stress and frustration. It's more than fine; it's inevitable. Surviving cancer or another life threatening illness does not give you a free pass from human problems for the rest of your time on earth (Wouldn't it be awesome if it did?). But remember, your illness journey has also given you an advantage. You know what it's like to go through some of the toughest suffering life can dish out, and you got through it. You have the tools to be happy and thankful in the worst circumstances, and the opportunity to apply that learning in a whole new, exciting phase. Your patience has paid off, your health has been restored, and you can *carpe the heck out of that diem,* in multiple ways:

- Remember: once a survivor, always a survivor. Your body is changed; you'll always bear the scars. But you'll always carry the experience and the lessons too.
- Live a dream. Seriously. If it sounds like a cliché, that's because we have to constantly remind each other that it is true. Fulfilling a wish isn't just for terminal patients. Pick something you've always wanted to do, do it, and enjoy every minute of the experience.
- Be available to others who go through this after you. I am still a member of the CTCL listserv. I post messages of encouragement to members who need support, offer sympathy to those who are down, and answer questions when my personal experience is relevant. I also speak at patient conferences and host online fundraisers. Whether you do it publicly or privately—whatever feels most comfortable for you—I encourage you to share your experience.

As a caregiver or supporter, your role doesn't necessarily end when the patient is in remission or cured. Here's how you can help at this stage:

- Become a donor. Get on the stem cell donor list, or give blood, or sign up for organ donation. It really does save lives.
- Invite them back into the world. Cancer patients sort of fall off the social radar while going through treatment. Remember what I said about feeling like Rip Van Winkle? Many survivors come back to the world feeling like it has passed them by and everyone else has moved on. Include them in invitations to parties and gatherings. Ask them to volunteer at church or civic events.

I am happy to say that Nancy and I have a normal life again. Is it exactly the same as the life we had before my CTCL diagnosis? Of course not. The experience changed both of us. Some wounds took a long time to heal—not just the physical ones in my body but the emotional and spiritual ones that arose from the stress, the family conflicts, and the occasions where people let us down. Additionally, I will always carry the memories of that dark time. So will my wife. I can't tell you how many times I've looked at her, or another person, and said, "I still can't believe we went through all that!" In the process of writing this book, I must have thought it dozens of times.

But here's the thing: we got through. And I can say, with complete sincerity, that it made me a better person. I have tried to tell my story in a way that provides both truth and hope to those who need it. If it helps you and your loved ones on your own cancer journey, then my own journey was worthwhile. My wish for you is that one day you too may step into the light of a warm day, raise your arms, and shout, "I feel better!"

"The moment one definitely commits oneself, then Providence moves too. All sorts of things occur to help one that would never otherwise have occurred...unforeseen incidents, meetings, and material assistance, which no man could have dreamed would have come his way."
– Johann Wolfgang Von Goethe

Notes

Notes

Final Thoughts

Oh so glad the worst is over
I can start flying now
My best days are right in front of me
Yeah and I am almost there
'Cause now I am free.
– Mary J. Blige, "The Living Proof"

If you're on a cancer journey, or you're supporting someone who is, you're going to have some really devastating days. There will be discomfort, pain, and suffering. There will be a lot of emotional and spiritual stress as well. What I really want you to take away from this book is: **Never give up. Even on the worst days, a positive mindset will get you through.** Hopefully, I have given you some tools to help you set your own positive intentions and build that mindset for yourself.

Most people have to go through one or more significantly challenging events or setbacks before they awaken fully to the present moment. For myself, in fewer than ten years, I was diagnosed with three rare and difficult diseases. Each one taught me something and helped me understand the importance of staying present to people and to all life has to offer. They taught me to recognize suffering in others.

So don't look at your health struggle—or any roadblock for that matter—as a nuisance. It may very well be the thing you need to experience to move you toward your greatness. In my opinion, God is always trying to get our attention. Usually it takes more than one or two exceptionally challenging life events before one says, "Wow, I finally get it! It's time for ME to wake up!" All of those annoying people, crummy jobs, and lousy circumstances that you thought were out to get you? They were really there to SERVE you.

Cancer will try to frighten you, paralyze you, and defeat you. You can't just wish it away, but you *can* control your attitude, keep moving forward, and strive for good health. No matter how bad you feel, allowing yourself to become distraught and traumatized will only make it harder. If you live in a place of pain and dread, terrified of the next treatment, the pain and discomfort will be that much worse.

Reliving unresolved conflicts from the past, or being fearful of what the future holds, only complicates your life, holds you back, and impedes your recovery. Real growth, healing, and change take constant faith and intense belief.

So, I encourage you to feed your positive intentions with the things that nourish and uplift you most. Do daily meditation, read your religious texts or inspirational authors, and listen to calming and uplifting music. Whatever feeds your soul and keeps mind friction in place, whatever kicks out the garbage, the negative thoughts, and the fear—do that! You need these things to maintain peace of mind and to manifest your desires and dreams.

I have always loved swimming; in the early days of my CTCL treatment, and starting about eight months after my transplant, I would swim laps at the gym. With every lap, I would choose a couple of positive phrases. With each stroke and kick, I would tell myself, "I am strong, I am healthy. I am strong, I am healthy. I am blessed, I am well. I am blessed, I am well."

Swimming was my quiet place, my space with no distractions. Find yours: somewhere away from your kids, your spouse or partner, or anyone else who demands your time and attention. Even if you live alone, you've got to find a way to quiet your mind, to get still, and develop mindfulness. Whether it's hiking in the woods, taking a yoga class, or finding the right meditation spot, finding and using that quiet space will help you to become more mindful in your everyday life.

I can't stress this enough. Your mind can be your greatest ally in the fight for your health, or it can be your worst enemy. It's not your doctors; it's not your spouse; it's not your kids; it's not people in your family. It's not even the disease. It's the story you tell yourself—the thoughts in your head that will defeat you or see you through.

Be kind to yourself. Don't fret or get down on yourself if it takes a while to cultivate your own feelings of peace and positivity. When you first start to practice mindfulness, especially if you're also undergoing cancer treatment, you're going to hear noise, noise, noise in your head. If you're like me, you'll find yourself saying, "Oh, my gosh! I had no idea I had so many negative thoughts running around in here!" Then you'll try forcefully to push them out...which only creates more mind friction. So, be gentle with yourself. Never give up.

You don't need to compare yourself to anybody else, because nobody else is right there in that exact moment with you. No one else has quite the cancer experience that you have. And you don't have to judge yourself for how good you are or are not. Just make the effort to be the best that you can be, on any given day. And that will lift you up and keep your personal demons at bay. Otherwise, you go to the dark side.

Even if it's just 30 minutes every day, try to spend some time getting in touch with your thoughts and feelings. With the greatest compassion, guide your mind toward positive intentions, and you'll find that will help dissipate the fear, increase your confidence, and boost your wellbeing.

Stay present, no matter what life circumstance you are experiencing; and, in time, you may just find a treasure on the other side of your suffering.

All my best,
Danna Wessels

"Illness is the night-side of life, a more onerous citizenship. Everyone who is born holds dual citizenship, in the kingdom of the well and in the kingdom of the sick. Although we prefer only to use the good passport, sooner or later each of us is obliged, at least for a spell, to identify ourselves as citizens of that other place."
— Susan Sontag

Notes

Notes

The Death Experience
Danna Wessels

There was a place. It was dark. It was mysterious. It offered a death experience.
People filed in, either alone or with someone, and told the proprietor which death experience they preferred.
The seeker had to state if they wanted a temporary death experience or a permanent death experience.
It was silent. It was cold. It was scary. I chose a temporary death experience.
There was one more choice that had to be made.
One could tell the death proprietor upon awakening from death if they wanted a hand sketched portrait of their dead self.
I requested such a portrait.
I quickly glanced in the direction where the portrait was to be found.
Not wanting to view this portrait
I ran through the death hallway
Out into the park
Beautiful trees
Twinkling water
Awake, Alive
The death proprietor nowhere to be found.

Appendix: Meditations and Exercises

For maximum benefit, meditation should be done in a quiet place where you feel comfortable and will not be disturbed. However, these meditations are short and simple enough that they can also be done whenever you feel a need for calm and peace, even if you're stuck in a busy, crowded, public environment.

Chapter 1: After Diagnosis

Meditation: Take a deep breath in. As you exhale, say to yourself, "I choose hope."
Take another deep breath in. As you exhale, say, "Choose hope."
Take another deep breath in. As you exhale, say, "Hope."

Repeat the sequence as many times as needed.

For Patients:

1. Name one activity you value or enjoy that you can choose to continue doing even when you are sick:

_____
_____
_____
_____

2. Describe how you would like your relationship and interactions with your medical professionals to go:

_____
_____
_____
_____

3. Name one thing you experience every day that makes you feel glad or grateful.

_____
_____
_____
_____

For Caregivers:

1. Name something that used to bother you or seem like a big deal—a burden, chore, or annoyance—that seems trivial after your loved one's diagnosis:

_____

_____

_____

_____

2. What is one small, nice thing you can do for yourself every day from now on?

_____

_____

_____

_____

Chapter 2: When Treatment Begins

Meditation: Find a place to sit or lie down. Take several long, slow breaths in this way: inhale for up to 10 seconds. Hold your breath for 3 seconds. Exhale as slowly and gently as you can. Once you have done this a few times, create a mental picture of your body's cells. (You can imagine them as actual cells, or something metaphorical like the buds of flowers or the bricks of a building). Imagine them becoming stronger, bigger, healthier, and whole.

Repeat the sequence as many times as needed.

For Patients:

1. Name one activity you value or enjoy that you can choose to continue doing even on days when you feel tired or ill:

_____
_____
_____
_____

2. Describe how you would like your relationship and interactions with your medical professionals to go:

_____
_____
_____
_____

3. Name one thing you experience every day that makes you feel glad or grateful

_____
_____
_____
_____

For Caregivers:

1. Name something that used to bother you or seem like a big deal—a burden, chore, or annoyance—that seems trivial after your loved one's diagnosis:

_____

_____

_____

_____

2. What is one small, nice thing you can do for yourself every day from now on?

_____

_____

_____

_____

Chapter 3: In Difficult Moments

Meditation: Think of a color you really dislike. Now think of the color you like best. Imagine your body as a container filled with the color you hate. Take a breath in. As you exhale, imagine that color starting to escape from your mouth and nose, starting with your feet. Imagine the empty space filling with your favorite color. Repeat the process of inhaling and exhaling until the *bad color* is totally replaced by the *good color,* from your head to your toes, and the container of your body is now filled with that shade you love.

(Note: this can be done while you are experiencing discomfort from a treatment, suffering other forms of physical distress, or feeling emotionally distressed about your current circumstances.)

For Patients:

1. What is your ideal *truth level?* How much detailed information about your illness and treatment is optimal for you?

_____
_____
_____
_____

2. What *whistle while you wait* activities can you enjoy right now?

_____
_____
_____
_____

3. Is there something in your treatment program, or life, that just stays hard? Write it here. Then, write a short poem about that thing, telling it how much it sucks. It can be serious, funny, or whatever tone you prefer.

_____

_____

_____

_____

For Caregivers:

1. Who is the ideal person to be the researcher and *keeper of information* about this illness and its treatment?

_____

_____

_____

_____

2. Name one thing, independent of your relationship to the patient, that comforts you when you feel stressed or scared. Commit to allowing yourself time and space to do this thing on days when you are frazzled or overwhelmed:

_____

_____

_____

_____

Chapter 4: In Recovery

Meditation: Say to yourself, "I am strong, I am healthy; I am strong, I am healthy; I am blessed, I am well; I am blessed, I am well." If you are still weak and resting constantly, you can open and close your hands or eyes as you repeat each phrase. If you are able enough for walking or gentle stretches, time each phrase to a step, movement, or breath.

For Patients:

1. Make a list of your favorite music, podcasts, audiobooks, or videos. Give that list to a caregiver, and have the items available to play on request:

_____

_____

_____

_____

2. What are your favorite vistas—views, like the ocean, penguins at the aquarium, a running stream, or cityscape at night? Write them below. Have someone set up a TV or computer screen that displays that vista, near your bed or chair. Apps and webcams are available to play these live or on a loop.

_____

_____

_____

_____

3. Find a notebook or put a sheet of paper on a wall. Each time you reach a milestone, or recover the ability to do something small, write down the date and the item.

_____

_____

_____

_____

For Caregivers:

1. What small, ordinary activity are you struggling to find time for as you provide care? Commit to asking someone to help you accomplish this small task once a week:

_____

_____

_____

_____

2. Make a list of very small, easy chores or responsibilities the patient could do with little effort. As they show improvement, start asking them to do these small things.

_____

_____

_____

_____

Acknowledgements

First, thanks to my beautiful wife, Nancy. I don't even know if it is possible to fully describe the challenges she faced during my cancer journey. She supported me through all of my treatments, faced my suffering with bravery and compassion, cleaned and sterilized constantly, and still showed up for work every day, even if that meant logging onto a laptop from our sofa. We're both grateful that she had such an understanding employer. I don't know how she balanced her job responsibilities and keeping me alive through those 100 days and beyond. No spouse could have done more than she did. She's my lifeline and my own personal enlightened warrior. I'm grateful for her love, her steadfast support, and of course, her potato soup.

Next, I owe my life to my other perfect match: the anonymous woman from the Netherlands, whose blood antigens matched mine, and who donated the stem cells used in my transplant. The international rules established by an overseas country indicate that we can't meet in person or talk directly, so she will always be something of a mystery. I don't know her name, or the city where she lives. I only know she must be an incredibly generous soul.

Thanks also to the members of the CTCL Listserv. In the days and weeks after my diagnosis, I was frightened and confused about having this rare disease. Within hours of my first post to the listserv, I had friendly, encouraging replies from people all over. As I interacted with patients who had been managing CTCL for 5, 10, or even 15 years, it gave me hope and confidence that I could survive too. That community meant so much to me through the various stages of my journey; often, I exchanged messages with list members on a daily basis. Their honesty, openness, and information got me through some tough times and helped me make the best decisions for my treatment. They also celebrated my recovery.

Susan Thornton, CEO of the Cutaneous Lymphoma Foundation, works tirelessly. I've had the honor, on many occasions, to be a speaker at the patient and physician conferences she so ably plans throughout the United States. Nearly every attendee I've met has had something wonderful to say about Susan and the work of the CLF.

I am indebted to the healthcare professionals who cared for me during those five years. Dr. Susan Dubois saved my life long before CTCL was in the picture. Dermatologist, Dr. Anne Epstein, wasted no time getting me a proper diagnosis when those red patches showed up. Drs. Madeleine Duvic and Han Myint supervise the treatment of many people each year, and strive to meet each one with individual attention and respect. Dr. M.'s honesty, patience, and sense of humor were invaluable as we progressed through an increasingly aggressive treatment regimen. R.N., Chris Taylor (formerly Koch), served as transplant coordinator for the University of Colorado hospital, was my liaison to Be the Match, and helped me find the perfect stem cell donor. I liked her from the first moment I met her. Her sensitivity and soft-spoken intelligence helped us so much during the difficult wait for a donor match. My gratitude also to the R.N., Michell Schaffer, whose antics with Miss Moo made photopheresis more bearable. She was such a vivacious, special, unique professional and beautiful human being. She was always laughing and making patients feel better. Unfortunately, she passed away from brain cancer some time ago, but I will always remember her with great fondness.

Thanks also go to my extended family, who were there cheering me on from the stands. My Mom checked in every week and prayed for me. My sister, Terri Coburn, came to stay and pitched in when Nancy was juggling so many responsibilities. My whole life, my mother's sister, Carolyn, has been more like an older sister than an aunt; she's

Acknowledgements

a beautiful soul, very giving and nurturing, who called and prayed for us through the whole ordeal. Her daughters—my cousins— Pam Vasquez and Kristi Booker, sent wonderful get-well cards. Carolyn and Kristi's presence was a wonderful surprise at our Grand Reception.

Kristi and Pam's kids—Katelyn, McKenna, Trenton, and Madelyn—made wonderful hand-drawn pictures. My cousin, John Wessels, came to Colorado with his wife, Debbie, during my post-transplant recovery. Their visit to our home touched me, brought me up to date on all the family news, and lifted my spirits. Aunt Pat Zwernemann understood cancer up-close-and-personal; she had cared for her first husband during his 10-year battle, and understood all that disease can take away and all it can burden you with. She and Uncle Herb sent bright, cheerful cards every month, and I always looked forward to her encouraging notes.

Special thanks to the spirits of our canine kids, corgis Gracie Belle and George Edward, for everything they did to make me feel better throughout the whole treatment process. After my transplant, that first 30 days at home without them were some of the longest of my life. Their curiosity, compassion, and companionship were the best medicine I received. We lost Gracie in 2015, and George in 2017, but they'll be in my heart always, and I look forward to meeting them on the Rainbow Bridge one day.

Siblings, Tara and Darren Green, were the best friends Gracie and George could have had during my illness. Darren opened his home, and Tara reorganized her schedule to look after them for well over a month. We're so grateful for the loving care they gave our canine kids. To our friend, Patty "Smart and Tall" Smart, and neighbor, Laura, on Lexington Street, thanks so much for driving me back and forth to TSEB appointments. It was a serious commitment of time and effort: 45 minutes travel each way, waiting up to 2 hours while I went through the procedure, and helping me drag my stinging, exhausted body back home after. That truly was above and beyond.

To Sherrie Stille, thanks for walking and feeding the dogs on days when our schedule was consumed by doctor's appointments and treatment. We so appreciated the peace of mind it gave us to know George and Gracie were in good hands, and we always enjoyed those photo updates sent to our smartphones.

Theresa and Vic Soto were true friends. As a fellow CTCL and stem cell transplant survivor, Theresa's support and advice were invaluable. Like Nancy, she was my lifeline, an MVP in my cancer battle. Neither she nor Vic could have been more supportive, driving me to appointments, staying with me while Nancy was out of town, making food runs when I felt like I could eat, and sitting with me in the emergency room. We might have butted heads sometimes, but they never let me down. God bless you.

Gail Gonzales, our good friend and graphic design/marketing guru, thank you for creating my beautiful book cover. It expresses my journey perfectly. Gail Gonzales can be reached at: gail@greatergoodgraphicdesign.com.

Finally, thanks to Carolyn D. Roark, "The Writing Texan," for helping me tell my story.

Resources

I found help, wisdom, and support in many places during my cancer journey. Some are listed below, and I encourage readers to seek them out.

I also encourage you to find your own creative outlets for processing and overcoming the emotional difficulties of a cancer battle. I have included some of my poems throughout the book as an example of how I processed some of my own thoughts and feelings. I hope you feel empowered to find the outlet that works best for you!

Web Resources:
CTCL List serv (online): CTCL-MF@LISTSERV.ACOR.org
Cutaneous Lymphoma Foundation: www.clfoundation.org
Diagnosis.com
Yale Cancer Center: www.yalecancercenter.org

Reading:
For self help, inspirational thinking, and spiritual awakening, I highly recommend the following authors. Many of these books focus on the law of attraction and the power of right intended thought, which I used daily when living with cancer and recovering from my Stem Cell Transplant.

Marc Allen
Maya Angelou
David Bach
Claude M. Bristol
Bill Bryson

Tony Burroughs
George S. Clason
Dr. Deepak Chopra
Walt Disney
Dr. Wayne Dyer
T. Harv Eker
Khalil Gibran
Doris Kearns Goodman
Thich Nhat Hanh
Napoleon Hill
Ernest Holmes
Michael J. Losier
Dan Millman
Toni Morrison
Alice Munro
Joseph Murphy
Norman Vincent Peale
Bob Proctor
Don Miguel Ruiz
Robin S. Sharma
Huston Smith
Zadie Smith
Gloria Steinem
Eckhart Tolle
Joe Vitale
Oprah Winfrey
Jon Kabat Zinn, Ph.D

Music
Listening to music, especially from these four artists, could physically remove severe stomach cramps and help me to transcend pain and go to sleep.

Mary J. Blige, *My Life II...the Journey Continues*, especially "The Living Proof."

Jason Raize, "Endless Night" from the *Lion King* soundtrack.
Carlos Nakai, flutist
Deva Premal, All of her CD's are centering/soulful, especially *The Essence.*

About the Author

Danna was born Dana Gay Wessels, on February 28, 1958, in a suburb of Northwest Houston. She and her younger sister, Terri, enjoyed a childhood of playing in the local park, hanging out with the kids on the block, and riding bicycles in the Mangum Manor neighborhood. She lived with her family in the same home from the time of her birth until her high school graduation in 1976.

Like many suburban Texas kids, Danna went off to college at the age of 18. After two years at Texas Tech, however, Danna realized she needed to find a direction for her life before setting on a degree plan. She returned to Houston, where she spent the next 3 years exploring different fields—including accounting, employment counseling, and personnel. At last, she realized her future lay in human resources, and she returned to college to finish her bachelor's degree in Organizational Psychology. She graduated from the University of Texas at Austin, in 1985.

Six years later, while working for the City of Austin, Danna encountered a stranger in the Two Commodore Plaza elevators: a genuine, charming woman with big brown eyes. This was Nancy, her future wife.

Meeting her soul mate certainly changed the shape of the next 10 years of Danna's life—in the best possible way! They supported each other in pursuing career success in human resources, explored the city's arts and culture scene, spent weekends exploring the Hill Country, built a home together with beautiful flower gardens, and raised Pembroke Welsh Corgis. If you ask, Danna will still say, "Meeting and falling in love with Nancy has been the absolute best thing that has ever happened to me."

Unfortunately, the next big changes would not be so welcome. In 1998, her father passed away. In December of the same year, Danna ended up in the emergency room with a mystery ailment that turned out to be the onset of Type 1 (Juvenile) Diabetes—not the Christmas present from life that anyone really hopes to receive. Nevertheless, Danna and Nancy stayed positive for the six months it took to learn to manage and live with the condition. The next major health hurdle for Danna was a 2004 diagnosis of Addison's disease. As a woman used to good health, who enjoyed lots of exercise and outdoor activity, it was sometimes difficult to overcome the feeling of being betrayed by her own body. Fortunately, meditation and mindset training were an important part of Danna and Nancy's life as a couple.

Perhaps these setbacks were dress rehearsals for the *big show,* the cancer journey chronicled by this book.

For the next major health milestone, shortly after the CTCL diagnosis, Danna & Nancy moved to Boulder, Colorado for Nancy's new job. As fate would have it Danna continued all of her treatments at The Anschutz Cancer Center and The University of Colorado Hospital on the same campus in Aurora, Colorado where she received her life saving Bone Marrow Transplant in June 2011.

Now, cancer free for 7+ years, and feeling great, Danna stays connected to the CTCL community and speaks at events for patients, caregivers, and medical professionals in the field. She and Nancy—now a married couple—make their home in south Austin, together with rescued dogs Jaxon and Finley.

Made in the USA
Coppell, TX
05 June 2022

78511883R00066